RELIGIOUS
REBELS

RELIGIOUS REBELS

FINDING JESUS IN THE AWKWARD MIDDLE WAY

CHRISTY LYNNE WOOD

credo
house publishers

Published in the United States of America by Credo House Publishers,
a division of Credo Communications LLC, Grand Rapids, Michigan
credohousepublishers.com

Some names, locations, and identifying characteristics have been changed
to protect the privacy of individuals.

Unless otherwise indicated, Scripture is taken from The Holy Bible,
English Standard Version, copyright © 2001 by Crossway Bibles,
a division of Good News Publishers. Used by permission. All rights reserved.

Scripture quotations marked (NIV) are taken from the Holy Bible,
New International Version®, NIV®. Copyright © 1973, 1978, 1984, 2011 by Biblica, Inc.™
Used by permission of Zondervan. All rights reserved.

Scripture marked (NKJV) is taken from the New King James Version®.
Copyright © 1982 by Thomas Nelson. Used by permission. All rights reserved.

Scripture quotations marked (KJV) are from the King James Version of the Bible.

ISBN: 978-1-62586-248-8

Cover and interior design by Sharon VanLoozenoord
Editing by Emily Irish

Printed in the United States of America
First edition

CONTENTS

INTRODUCTION

If you are holding this book, then you've probably been on your own journey of doubt. I'm guessing you have a lot of questions. Maybe like me, you've been labeled a rebel. Perhaps you've experienced religious trauma and spiritual abuse. And yet, despite everything you've been through, you can't give up on Jesus. You hold on to hope that He exists, and that what you've experienced with Him is real on some level.

You might find yourself questioning the traditions of religious Christianity. Perhaps you are cynical about the corporate church and that cynicism only grows every time another leader is exposed for being a fraud, abuser, or worse. Maybe you are exhausted by a feeling that you can never measure up to Christian expectations. If this describes you, then you are in the right place.

Don't be ashamed of your doubts and questions. Or afraid of your cynicism and the snarky attitude that simmers beneath the surface when it comes to organized religion. Don't feel guilty because of your frustration and disillusionment with Christianity. I have good news for us. We want more because there is more. We are disillusioned because we've found a fake substitute. Our cranky hearts are leading us home.

I spent a decade in a Christian cult full of rules, lies, and twisted Scripture. I was the good girl following along until one day Jesus showed up and changed everything. As I got to know

Jesus for myself, I began to realize that the God I knew and the god I was being taught about couldn't be the same Person.

My search for the real Jesus has led me to a space of paradox, tension, and mystery where I'm learning to embrace uncertainty even as I hold onto truth. I don't seem to fit into any of the neat categories or sides of arguments. I'm often too progressive for conservatives and too orthodox for progressives. Maybe you can relate, and maybe like me, you feel a bit lost. Welcome to what I call the Awkward Middle Way, to the of band religious rebels. I'm glad you are here, and I hope that this book gives you a place where you can belong.

PART ONE
BECOMING A REBEL

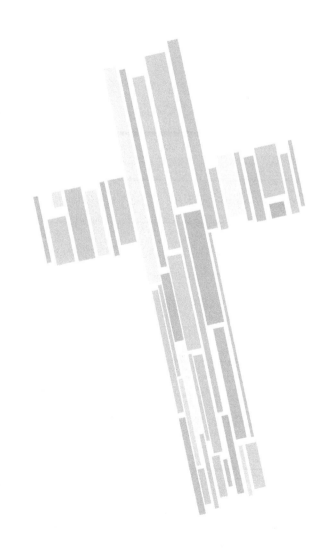

1

BEGINNINGS OF REBELLION

I think I've been brainwashed. The unexpected thought pierced my sleepy fog. It was after midnight, but all of us girls had been dragged from our sleeping bags for a special lecture. Clumped together on a couple of ratty old couches, we yawned and tried to listen. I was all too aware that my alarm was going off in less than six hours. Prayer meeting started at 6:30 a.m., and if I cared about giving off a spiritual vibe, then I needed to be there. Which meant getting up even earlier to shower, blow-dry, and curl my hair, because for some reason curly hair was also a sign of spirituality.

Mrs. W droned on and on about cliques and friendship, and I felt myself drifting off. Then she said it, the real reason this meeting had been called.

"It just grieved my heart, to look out the window earlier and see you all playing in the snow. I couldn't tell who the boys were and who the girls were since you were all wearing snow pants." Her voice dripped with judgmental disappointment.

It was true. At this winter youth retreat, we were all wearing snow pants while we played in the snow. But it was shocking, and apparently deserving of a midnight lecture, because in previous years most of us girls, or at least the godly ones, had worn skirts or culottes over our snow pants to preserve our femininity.

How do I explain culottes? The first ones we wore were homemade and looked like an awkwardly full, calf-length skirt. However, unlike a skirt, if you grabbed the sides and pulled, voilà, there were two sections of fabric, one for each leg. Over the years, our culottes shrank down to a slightly larger version of modern gaucho pants. We wore them when a skirt was a safety hazard, such as swimming, horseback riding, or downhill skiing. Downhill skiing in culottes, even skinnier ones, is a bit like skiing with two flags attached to your legs. I can still feel them streaming behind me flapping wildly in the wind.

The ridiculousness of it all sank in. We had been dragged from our warm beds in the middle of the night to be lectured about modesty because we had failed to put another layer of clothing on top of our already-poofy snow pants.

I rested my head on the shoulder of the girl next to me and stared skeptically at the woman lecturing us. An increasingly familiar feeling of rebellion crept over me. I had always been a good girl—one of the godly ones—but that was changing. And surprisingly enough, it wasn't rock music, or blue jeans, or college that was turning me into a rebel (like we'd been warned about). It was Jesus.

⁕ ⁙ ⁙ ⁙ ⁕

Do you have a moment like this? When the lights turned on, the questions started, and the rebellion began? Or maybe it was a thousand little moments that ultimately led to one big bang—the scary realization that *I don't believe this anymore.* My story might be on the extreme side of things, but I know that the questions I've asked and the doubts I've faced are common.

The lies I learned in my Christian cult have twisted their way into mainstream churches, books, and sermons. They are familiar lies not tied to one organization or leader but spread across many versions of Christian religion. They are behavior-driven lies that are motivated by fear and used to control. And while many times these lies claim to be backed up with Bible verses and even use the name of God or Jesus, they are not actually truths spoken by Him.

When I first began to deconstruct my faith, it wasn't even a word people were using. I just knew that it was necessary to dissect the beliefs from my Christian cult, look at them closely, go to Scripture, talk to the Jesus I knew, and determine what was false, twisted, or true. It was something I had to do. Maybe you feel that urgency too.

I've gone through four major seasons of faith deconstruction in my life so far, and most of them happened before the phrase became popular. But each time I have rebuilt my beliefs around the actual Word of God and the very real Being who found me when I wasn't even looking. You will hear more about this later in this book.

Deconstruction is a buzz word these days and unfortunately, like everything else in our society, it has become polarized. People seem quick to form black-and-white opinions about both the process of deconstruction and those who experience it. Some people condemn all deconstruction because they feel it is dangerous and fear that it always leads to apostasy. Other people celebrate it but then assume everyone who deconstructs will automatically come to see the world and faith from their more progressive point of view. Although opinions about the process are often rigid, deconstruction itself is kind of a cloudy term that can mean totally different things to different people. Let's see if we can make it clearer.

Apart from the faith context, to deconstruct something means to take it apart to its individual components. We can deconstruct buildings, cocktails, clothes, hamburgers, and more. After something is taken apart, the carpenter, mixologist, designer, or chef often analyzes the pieces and then reinterprets them in a new and different way. The process of faith deconstruction shouldn't be condemned because at its core, it is just taking the Christian religion apart and analyzing the individual components. Let me give you an illustration.

Pretend with me that there was this incredible Lego set. Over the years people added pieces to it—most of them with the best intentions. They were trying to make it look defined, creative, and better designed. But after a while people couldn't tell what the set originally looked like. It was just a pile of Lego blocks stuck together. This is what has happened with our modern Christianity.

I took the blocks apart and separated the pieces. Then I looked at the instructions—which were kind of crumpled and hard to read. I tried to choose the blocks that belonged to the original set and did my best to follow the directions even though they weren't always easy to decipher. I put the Lego set back together again and threw the extra blocks in my tote. This is my faith deconstruction and reconstruction story.

Not everyone deconstructs this way, but because we use the same word to describe our journeys, it can be confusing. Some people separate the blocks and then use them to build something completely different. The end results can vary drastically. Other people take the blocks apart and throw them in the trash or leave them in a pile on the floor and walk away for a while or forever.

We all took the pieces apart, so we all call what we did with them deconstruction. But it's what happened after we took them apart that makes our stories so different. It creates a complicated definition because deconstruction means different things to each of us. If we could just agree that deconstruction means taking something apart down to its individual components, then maybe we could stop condemning or making assumptions.

"Christy, why are you still a Christian?" My friend, who happened to be an atheist, stared at me intently from across the room.

It was a valid question, and one I had been pondering myself. Over ten years had passed since that midnight lecture on the couch, ten years and countless life changes. I was a youth pastor's wife and mother of two. I wore jeans every day, had a bachelor's degree from a secular college, and listened to a playlist with drums in every song. People in my current life knew that I had been homeschooled, but even my husband was oblivious to the extent of crazy I'd experienced in our cultic subgroup of Christianity.

Shortly after realizing I might have been brainwashed, I spent a summer working at a Christian camp. Showing up with my ankle-length skirts and waist-length hair, I had a mile-long list of rules and standards. But those normal Christians—people I had been told were worldly—loved Jesus. And they loved and accepted me in a way I'd never felt before. I found freedom in those ten, beautifully wild weeks. Freedom, grace, and life. At the end of the summer, I got a cartilage piercing to remind me of my newfound freedom in Jesus.

My old friends weren't impressed. Getting chased through Cedar Point—literally running—to avoid their attempt to lecture me about my poor life choices was the tipping point. I shut the door on that part of my life. It was pretty easy since my family was no longer closely associated with our church group or organization. I went to college, met an amazing man who was my total opposite, dated and married him, and left the old me behind.

But now the door to my past was beginning to crack open. I learned that the man we previously respected and followed was being accused of sexual harassment with multiple girls over decades. I discovered a website dedicated to exposing truth about the cultic organization my family was a part of through my teens and early twenties. I found online support groups filled with former students like me. These discoveries confirmed things I had always suspected. The floodgates opened.

My poor husband listened patiently to many rants, frustrations, and memories. I sorted through truths and lies. I connected and reconnected with people who shared an understanding of my crazy past. It was exciting, healing, and heartbreaking.

The number of people who grew up like me but left Christianity completely was overwhelming. I understood in theory. If what we had experienced was the real God, then no wonder they wanted nothing to do with Him. But it made me sad, and it made me question.

Why was I still a Christian? Why hadn't I run away too? I knew why.

I'd met Jesus. And while I rejected the legalism, ridiculous standards, and performance-driven faith, I couldn't reject Him. Because I loved Him, and I knew that He loved me. It was worth the fight. It was worth deconstructing and reconstructing my faith to find the real God.

❚|❚■❚|■

I think many Christians accept a fake version of Jesus without even realizing it, whether they grew up in a cult or not. We speak fluent Christianese, using familiar words and phrases without thought. We follow traditions and believe supposed truth because that is what we were taught. We have black-and-white answers for everything, and the god of our theology is small, understand-able, and containable. But if you're like me, deep within our hearts we find ourselves disillusioned and cranky. What is wrong with us? Why isn't this Christianity thing working? Why do we feel such shame and condemnation? What made us so cynical? Why can't we get it together?

I have a crazy thought. What if our cranky, disillusioned hearts are leading us home? Could it be that the Spirit is mov-ing within us and the discontentment is from Him? What if we rejected our religious Christianity and began a hunt for the real Jesus? It's scary to let go of what you think you know. Sometimes it's downright terrifying. But if God is real, and if He wants to be found, then we will be okay.

The truth is, our modern Christianity desperately needs this deconstruction movement. And it isn't anything new. Believers have been rethinking their faith and the beliefs of the corporate church for almost two thousand years. It started with Jesus and continued with the apostle Paul, Martin Luther, Saint Augustine, Dietrich Bonhoeffer, C. S. Lewis, et al. Not everyone got everything right obviously, but they all pushed back against lies of their day in a search for truth.

As broken humans, we are quick to misunderstand and misrepresent God. We all think we are right, but we also all tend to love power, money, and fame. Sin has skewed our perspective. There's an awful lot of corruption and abuse within the church that has been exposed recently, and while it's heartbreaking, it isn't new. The revelation that sinful humans have abused their power and twisted God's Word doesn't make Him or it less real or powerful. It just gives us a new opportunity to question, ponder, and explore.

This book is an adventure filled with bits and pieces of my own journey to find truth and reconstruct my beliefs. It is a reminder that Jesus didn't fit into the religious systems of his day either. And it is an invitation for you to dig into your own questions, fears, and doubts. I'm here to tell you that those questions and doubts are okay. It is good to take apart your faith and beliefs to search for truth. Your skepticism is valid. You are not a bad person because of your doubts.

This book is also the story of how I've reconstructed my faith centered around Scripture and the person of Jesus Christ. Not the twisted, out-of-context Bible verses that I grew up with, but Scripture as it was meant to be read: as a whole, according to its genre, and keeping in mind things like culture and author intent. We will talk more about this in a coming chapter. The Jesus I follow today is not the same Jesus I grew up with. I can't wait to tell you that story. Thanks for being here. I'm excited to have you join me as we rethink the Christianity we grew up with while trying to navigate the Awkward Middle Way of grace and truth.

OUR DOUBTS AND QUESTIONS ARE JUST THE BEGINNING.

HINTS OF DOUBT

Kneeling by the bunk bed I shared with my sister, I whispered
a prayer. "God, you are Jehovah Jireh, you always provide for us.
You are El Roi, you see everything. You are Jehovah Shammah,
you are always there." My fingers traced the stitching in the quilt
as I read from the paper in my hand. It was a homeschool assignment, believe it or not, and I was fifteen years old.

"Go and pray this list of God's names," my mom had told me.
And I dutifully began to pray, unaware that my entire life was
about to change.

In the middle of my quiet prayer, I suddenly realized that
I was not alone. A very real, very large Presence was with me,
listening to and enjoying my praise. It was unexpected, shocking,
and slightly terrifying. I don't remember if I finished the list or
not. I do know I jumped up and ran downstairs to my mother,
screaming, "Mom, Mom, God showed up!"

She smiled a knowing little smile and said, "I've been praying
that would happen."

I don't remember a time when I didn't believe in God and Jesus. I grew up in church with all the familiar Bible stories. I participated in Bible Quiz, went to church camp, and loved sword drills. God was as familiar to me as grilled cheese and tomato soup. He was a part of my life that I accepted but didn't really think about.

Childhood was pretty idyllic. My siblings and I grew up in rural Michigan on an old farm. We were raised in a beautifully old-fashioned way, with summers spent climbing trees, playing cops and robbers, and swinging on the rope swing in our hundred-year-old barn. My mom homeschooled us before it was an acceptable thing, and my dad taught at a local public school. Strange, I know. But life was good.

I've always been a people pleaser. Even as a child, I wanted to know the expectations so that I could follow them and make people like me. By the time I was fifteen, my family had gotten caught up in a cultic homeschool organization and a church filled with rules and religious legalism. I performed with the best of them. I had daily devotions, memorized Bible passages, followed the rules, and was always ready to answer the question, What is God doing in your life? But it was two-dimensional knowledge to me.

Although I believed in Him without question, God was a name on the page of an old book. He was a concept that I accepted and tried to appease. Now, surprisingly, God had jumped off the page and become a real and living Being. If God was more than a name, if He was a real Person, then I wanted to know Him. My spiritual life became transformed. I started looking for God in my Bible readings. I started praying to Him instead of at Him.

I began taking long walks to talk with Jesus. An access road for the farm fields ran along the edge of our yard. I can still hear the screen door slamming shut behind me as I ran out to walk that road with Jesus. I'd return thirty minutes later with the bottom half of my skirt wet from the dewy grass. Those are precious memories. Jesus was always there for me, and I started to recognize just how much He loved me. Ultimately, this real Jesus would lead me to question the god, the standards, and the rules my church and organizational leaders were telling me to follow.

What if God isn't who we think He is? What if God cares more about our heart than our outward actions? What if He wants to heal our deepest wounds and messes more than He wants our behaviors to change?

What if He wants us to understand ourselves—our deep needs, our longings, and the things that trigger us? What if He cares about every bit of us, the visible and invisible parts? What if, instead of expecting us to get our act cleaned up, Jesus wants to sit with us in our mess, sift through it, and sort it out? What if He is totally okay with that? What if that brings Him joy? Would that give you hope?

My heart longs for that kind of God with a yearning that brings tears to my eyes. Could it be true? More than anything I want this kind of God to exist. And if He does, well, that changes everything.

There are people in every church and denomination who are going through the motions of Christianity. They believe the correct theology and do the right behaviors, but instead of a give-and-take relationship, they have a flat, two-dimensional religion. Religious Christianity is enough for some people, but many others are packing up and leaving. I have met many people—both online and in person—who have walked away from corporate church and the faith they were raised in. Maybe that's you. And if it is, I understand. Religion alone does not provide good enough reasons to stay.

There is a lot of talk within evangelical Christianity about the decline of the church. Attendance is down, less people are identifying as Christians, and younger generations continue to be an elusive commodity. There have been multiple studies done and books written as people try to solve the problem. I'd like to throw out a theory: what if people are leaving because they have only met a religious impostor and not the real Jesus?

Maybe like me, you are tired of empty tradition, rules, and passive religion. Maybe you also are over condemnation, judgment, and hypocrites. It's not enough to simply get away from strict fundamentalism with big, fancy church buildings filled with talented bands, dynamic speakers, and smoke machines. We don't want more programs, fancy lattes, or feel-good sermons any more than we want "that old-time religion."

We want to ask hard questions and search for answers in a safe place of acceptance and friendship. We want honesty and truth, to be known and to know others. We want a God who is huge, unexpected, and real. We want to meet Jesus.

Four years after I felt God's presence for the first time, I was struggling. Something crazy was happening to me. I had always been the good girl, the people pleaser, and the godly example, but I was quickly becoming a rebel. It wasn't the forewarned evils of jeans, rock music, or college that was changing me either; it was Jesus. I paced back and forth on the sandy path with the sun filtering through the trees, trying to reconcile two opposing gods.

Our cultic church spent a week together every summer at family camp. We completely engulfed a Christian camp in northern Michigan and filled it with large, homeschooled, uber-conservative families. Cabins were filled to the brim, and there were tents and campers everywhere. Females walked around in skirts or culottes, ankle socks, and tennis shoes, while the males dressed in collared shirts and khakis with a trusty multipurpose tool attached to their belts. We held old-fashioned camp meetings two or three times a day in a huge white rental tent, where we sang hymns accompanied by a piano—because drums were evil—and listened to sermons. As a teenager, it was an amazing week, mostly because we got to spend so much time with other young people, especially members of the opposite sex.

That year, we began the week with a speaker who was a Messianic Jew. He talked about the power of Jesus Christ living in us. His God was incredibly real and personal, and the Jesus he spoke about resonated with me. In the four years since God showed up in the middle of my prayers, I had gotten to know Him as a genuine friend. This man confirmed what I had come to believe. Unfortunately, we had another speaker for the second half of the week.

This man, well-known in fundamental circles, gave us endless lists of rules to follow, impossible standards to uphold, and promises of God's blessings only if we followed them all. And that's when I lost it. His message made me sick. Listening to him put a bitter taste in my mouth, and I could hardly stand sitting in chapel. During the first half of the week, I sat near the front with other godly teens. But by the end of the week, I found myself slouched in the very back with the rebels, my arms crossed, unable to keep the grouchy look off my face. What was happening to me? This is *not* who I used to be.

My internal conflict brought me to the sandy path, walking back and forth and trying to reconcile the Jesus I'd been getting to know with the god my church and organization had been teaching me about for the past seven years. There was the Jesus who loved me and wanted a relationship with me, who gave me His Holy Spirit who empowered me to follow Him. Then there was the Jesus who gave rules, steps, and formulas and expected performance before he would bless you. They couldn't both be Jesus. One of them had to be a fake.

I got in tons of trouble that week at camp. Me, the former good girl. I had a blatantly rebellious attitude. I started questioning standards, such as why we wore skirts. I held fingertips with a boy while we were acting as romantic interests in a play about John Newton, the author of "Amazing Grace." It was scandalous.

People were confused. I'd always been such an example for others to follow. More than one adult confronted me, attempting to return me to the path of righteousness. But I was disillusioned, and I was done. There had to be more, and I was determined to find it.

What about you? Are you satisfied with the God people have taught you about? With the God you think might exist? With the religion you've experienced? These can be scary questions to ask. And even scarier questions to answer honestly. It's terrifying to think we might be losing our faith. But what if the doubt, frustration, and confusion we feel (or maybe try not to feel) isn't wrong? That disillusionment might be the Spirit calling us to something else. It could be the starting place to finding Someone bigger and crazier than we could ever imagine.

Guess what? I think it's okay to lose your faith. It doesn't make you a bad person. If our faith is based on a religious impostor and not the real God, then we need to lose that faith.

The real God is open to our doubts and questions. He wants us to ask them. He wants us to seek, and wrestle, and discover for ourselves who He really is in all of His insanity, and goodness, and power. How do I know this? Because it is a huge theme in the Bible. It is God's heart.

The prophet Jeremiah encouraged the Israelites to seek God even while in captivity, and he promised them that they would find Him when they sought with all their heart (Jeremiah 29:12–14). The apostle Paul used an altar to the unknown god in Athens to tell the people about a God so real that they could feel their way toward Him blindfolded and still find him (Acts 17:27–28). And Jesus himself reminded the crowds to ask, seek, and knock with the promise that they would receive and find the door open (Matthew 7:7–8).

God has promised repeatedly that if we search for Him, we will find Him. You will find Him. God created us to be in a relationship with Him. Jesus died to restore that friendship. Jesus wants us to know Him.

Is there a tiny bit of hope flickering in your heart? It is my desire and prayer that this book will fan that flame of hope and give you courage to ask, seek, knock, and find. I know that church can hurt deeply. Christians can cause unspeakable pain. But that's not Jesus. Jesus came to give us life. The real enemy is religion.

GOD MIGHT NOT BE WHO WE THINK HE IS, AND THAT'S OKAY.

3

PROBLEMS OF RELIGION

I lay on the floor of our bedroom, sobbing. Never had I felt such desperation and emptiness. There were no words even to pray. My beautiful little world had fallen completely apart. I was confused, hurt, and betrayed. And it was there in my brokenness that Jesus began to connect the dots.

Dealing with my decade of Christian-cult craziness didn't happen until after both of my children were born. Before that time, I had either shut the lid on my past or tried to normalize it. Picking through twisted truth to find the real Jesus was challenging, painful, and confusing. I felt like I was peeling an onion. Every time I worked through a layer, there was another layer underneath.

While initially processing my own experiences, I found a couple of online communities filled with former students who had been a part of the same cultic organization. Many of the people in these communities were questioning—and often abandoning—the concept of God and the Christian faith. Although it was nice to find others who understood what I'd gone through, and I enjoyed being involved in dialogue, I was also overwhelmed by the negativity toward Jesus.

Three books came out right about this time, and my online communities were excited about them. They were *Faith Unraveled* by Rachel Held Evans, *Girl at the End of the World* by Elizabeth Esther, and *When We Were on Fire* by Addie Zierman. Although I hadn't read them personally, these books made me angry. From what I heard online, I felt like I knew the premise. Each book was a memoir written by a woman who grew up in some form of evangelical Christianity but then had questioned or left the faith. It frustrated me that so many people were accepting what I felt were lies about God and abandoning Christianity. I sort of understood, but if I'm honest, I also had this attitude of "I made it out and I still love Jesus. Why can't you?" Then God let my world fall apart and I finally got it.

My husband and I lived through the hardest, most painful year of our lives due to conflict and spiritual abuse that happened within our church where he worked as a youth pastor. Some of the things that occurred triggered emotions and memories from my teens. I reexperienced rejection, condemnation, and despair that left me sobbing on my bedroom floor.

Making sense of the craziness from my past when I was in an isolated subculture of Christianity was easier. This hurt was coming from Christians who looked normal and should have been safe. Truthfully, if I hadn't met Jesus for myself, and if I didn't know who He really was, I might have left Christianity too. I thought about it. When you experience deep, dark pain in the name of Christ, it's easier to shove everything off the table and move on.

Strangely, broken desperation isn't necessarily a bad thing when the real Jesus is involved. I was humbled, raw, and feeling deep loss when I ordered three books from Amazon that December afternoon. I bought the books I thought I hated: *Faith Unraveled, Girl at the End of the World,* and *When We Were on Fire.* In my place of brokenness, I was ready to hear other people's stories about the hurt they had experienced within Christianity. I was ready to learn from people that I thought I disagreed with.

I ended up loving those books, even if the authors and I didn't come to all the same conclusions. I identified with their questions and pain. They reminded me of how messed-up our modern version of Christianity has become all cross the board. And even though they each had a unique story to tell, there were definite similarities. From Christian cults to evangelical youth groups, I saw a common theme. Every one of those authors was fed a fake, hurtful version of Jesus within a system of religious Christianity. That resonated with me on a deep-in-my-gut level.

As I processed my story alongside these women's experiences, I started to recognize connections between lies I had been taught and issues within the mainstream evangelical church. My initial thought was that our cultic organization had more influence than I'd ever imagined. But, the more I read, talked, and studied, the more I began to see a much larger problem.

If you look closely, you will find the same issues in small ultra-fundamental churches, mission organizations led by a narcissistic leader, or mega-churches with a charismatic but sometimes frightening senior pastor. The common denominator across different churches and organizations is an obsession with behavior-driven religion. Broken people pursue power and control and often use religion to make it happen. This is something that has been exposed again and again in recent years.

Some of the greatest examples of God versus religion are the many interactions between Jesus and the Pharisees in the Gospels. Reading these stories always amazes me. The Jewish leaders had their outward act together. They'd memorized the first five books of the Old Testament by the time they were twelve. They followed a gazillion rules. And they knew an abundance of information about Jehovah. Yet somehow, they still missed God walking in front of them, doing miracles, and speaking words of truth.

They not only failed to recognize Jesus as God but also despised Him enough to plot His death. Apparently being religious doesn't automatically connect you to God. How crazy is that?

At its core, religion is primarily about power and control. Being religious ourselves makes us feel like we are in control. Teaching other people how to appease God puts us in a position of power. Unfortunately, not only does religion wound and destroy people, it also ultimately keeps us from the real Jesus. The Pharisees focused on behavior and condemned others as sinners. They loved power and wanted to control those around them. Jesus—the real God—stood right in front of them, refused to play along, exposed their sinful hearts, and became their enemy.

I recently heard a great definition of the difference between power and authority. When a person has power, they can make people do what they want. But when a person has true authority, they live a life that people automatically want to follow. The religious Pharisees had power, but Jesus had genuine authority.

It's the power part of religious Christianity that usually hurts people. If you are reading this and have been wounded by something or someone that used the name of Jesus, I can almost guarantee it's because they were grasping for power instead of living out of true authority. That pain that you experienced was a result of broken religion, but it wasn't the real Jesus. Jesus didn't come to condemn or reject us. He came to restore us to the Father (John 3:17–18).

She stood there silently, her head bowed in shame. They wanted to stone her. And according to the law, those religious leaders had every right. She'd been caught in the very act of adultery. But they were using her as a test, and now they waited to see what the young rabbi would say.

He didn't say anything, simply knelt down next to her and began to write with his finger in the dirt. She saw his hand out of the corner of her eye and felt his presence next to her. He ignored the clamoring crowd and was silent as he drew. Finally, he stood. "Any of you who are without sin can be the first to throw a stone at her." Again, he knelt next to her and quietly wrote in the dirt with his finger. That was it. There was an awkward silence.

After a moment, she noticed that the crowd seemed smaller. Peering through her hair, she realized that the religious men were slowly leaving. Eventually, it was her and Jesus alone on that dusty patch of earth. He looked at her. She lifted her head. "Woman, where are they? Has no one condemned you?" His voice was kind. She looked around; they were all gone.

"No one, sir."

"I don't condemn you either." He smiled. "Go, and from now on sin no more."

This account of Jesus and the woman caught in adultery comes from John chapter eight. I love it because I can identify with that woman. I have been judged by religious people and religious institutions. I know what it feels like to face condemnation so strong that you don't see a way out. Maybe you've been there too. Your behavior hasn't measured up to the Christianese expectations and now you are doomed.

In a spectacular showdown between God and religion, Jesus completely blows everyone's mind. He refuses to play the Pharisees' game. Although He acknowledges the law, He also turns it on the accusers. Then He shows scandalous mercy and grace to an obvious sinner. If Jesus is God, shouldn't He be following the rules? Where does this ridiculous grace and mercy come from? Straight from the heart of the real God. It might sound crazy, but I'm pretty sure that the One who wrote the rules can decide how and when they should be applied.

It's easy to point fingers at people who have hurt us and call them religious, but the problems with religion are also intensely personal. It's my own pride and desire for control that makes religion attractive to me. You've probably heard the Christianese phrase, *It's not a religion; it's a relationship.* Ideally that should be true. But too often the same people who proclaim that concept turn around and hand others a list of good Christian behaviors. *If you really are in a relationship with Jesus, then this is what it should look like.* I don't know about you, but I've handed other people lists, and I've definitely made them for myself. That's not a relationship, that's religion.

Mike Cosper, author of *Recapturing the Wonder*, defines it this way: "Religion is the business of appeasing gods." I love this definition. Obviously, most of us don't have a little god shelf at home where we burn incense and offer sacrifices. But how often do we focus on our good behaviors as a means of appeasing God? Most of the time it's a subtle, automatic response. In our broken-ness, we are naturally religious. We do good to make God happy with us. We feel guilt over our bad and avoid Him. Where did this natural tendency toward religious behavior come from? It started in the very beginning.

⸭⸭⸭

"You won't really die," the serpent hissed. "God knows that when you eat it, your eyes will be opened. You will be like God, knowing about good, and evil." What the serpent said made sense. Maybe Adam and Eve were confused; maybe they had misunderstood God's original instructions. The fruit was beautiful to look at, and it would make them more like God. Why would God keep this knowledge from them? Surely, eating the fruit was the right thing to do. Forgetting they were already made in God's image, and thinking they were becoming more like Him, Adam and Eve listened to the serpent's words.

Feelings of guilt and shame flooded their souls with instant regret. With a jolt and a shiver, Adam and Eve recognized for the first time that they were naked. Frantically looking around, they snatched some large leaves and roughly fashioned them into coverings. Unfamiliar emotions churned sickeningly inside their stomachs. They knew that something deep within their souls had cracked. If this wasn't bad enough, Adam and Eve suddenly heard a sound that filled them with terror. It was a familiar noise that used to bring them joy. But now, hearing His footsteps coming closer, they searched desperately for a hiding spot.

Religion entered the world in Genesis chapter three, and it's been keeping us from the real God ever since. In response to their nakedness and shame, Adam and Eve did and hid. They covered their naked bodies by sewing together some fig leaves. Then, hearing the sound of God's footsteps, they hid from Him. This is the essence of religious behavior. Feeling shame over our broken-ness, we focus on doing things to try and fix ourselves. Convinc-ing ourselves that God is disappointed and angry, we hide from God rather than running to Him.

I really believe that religion, more than anything, is the true enemy of God, especially within Christianity. It's subtle. It dis-tracts. It makes us believe we have effort to offer, and it takes away from the beauty and wonder of the free gift. Religion turns a life-giving friendship into dutiful servanthood.

As He walked through the garden, God knew exactly what had happened moments before. He knew that Adam and Eve had doubted Him, believed a lie, and disobeyed His one command. But God came to them with a question rather than condemna-tion: "Where are you?" This is incredibly significant. It's the first glimpse that the real God is different from the god we expect. Yes, if we continue reading Genesis chapter three, we will see just con-sequences for Adam and Eve's sin, but we will also find ridiculous grace and mercy. This isn't religion; this is something else.

God has sought His people from the beginning, and God is still seeking today. If we could believe that, I think our spiritual life might be completely different. It's not like the fall surprised God. He knew exactly what would happen when He breathed out the universe only two chapters before. So, why did He do it? I don't know, and that's okay. God is bigger, crazier, and better than we will ever comprehend. The real God does not always make sense. His mystery is one of the beauties I have come to appreciate most about Him.

∎∎∎∎∎∎∎

The god I grew up with in my version of religious Christianity was explainable and predictable. There were answers with attached verses for every acceptable question. Unacceptable questions were shut down or ignored. Theology was cut and dried. But the more I have come to know the real God, the more I have realized how much I don't know. I have more questions now than I did when I started, but I'm also far more comfortable with not having answers.

I was talking with a friend recently. This person has experienced normal conservative Christianity, crazy cultic Christianity, and a variety of denominations in between. As we talked, she asked, "How do you know who is right? Everyone thinks they are right, but I'm not sure if any of us are really right about God."

"I'm not sure if any of us are really right about God." What if this is true? What if that's okay? Religious Christianity is often quick to give pat answers and even quicker to shut down uncomfortable questions. But what if the questions are good? What if it is more about the hunt, the search, than it is about finding the perfect right answer?

∎∎∎∎∎∎∎

As humans, we are naturally obsessed with behaviors. We create categories of perceived right and wrong, and then we judge other people based on how they perform. It's not just ultra-conservative people who do this either. You can have a completely liberal list of expected behaviors and condemn others because they don't meet your expectations. We struggle to get down to the heart of it all, to see people for who they are and not for how they act. I'm as guilty of this as anyone else.

In the Gospels, Jesus didn't really pay attention to people's behaviors. Instead, he asked questions that went straight to their hearts. He understood that right and wrong aren't always clearly defined. Jesus saw through the Pharisees' religious facade and called them whitewashed tombs. Then He turned around and made sinners His closest companions. This is the real God.

All religion, Christian or other, is human attempts to take care of, or distract from, our brokenness through our own efforts. God is not religion. He is above and beyond it. He sees straight through our behaviors to our hearts. He is truth and justice, and at the same time, lavish mercy and grace. God offers hope and love, undeserved and unearned. Because He wants to.

RELIGION IS AN ATTEMPT TO DEAL WITH OUR BROKENNESS BY OURSELVES. THE REAL GOD SEES PAST OUR BEHAVIORS AND SEEKS OUR HEARTS.

WORDS OF GOD

*This chapter is about the Bible, and I recognize that it may be a diffi-
cult chapter to read. It's okay. And it's okay if you don't know what you
think about the Bible right now, or if you can't read it, or if you don't.
This topic can be really triggering because the Bible has been used by
many to control and abuse people. It is my hope that this chapter will
help to remind us all of what the Bible is and what it isn't.*

There was no way it was going to happen. My stress level was
at an all-time high as I recognized the hard truth that I would
not meet the due date for this assignment unless something
drastically changed. Fresh out of homeschooled high school, and
because my subculture rejected traditional college education, I
was pursuing some online college-like classes through our cultic
institute. The constant stress of assignments, deadlines, and a
never-satisfied English teacher was hard enough, but the impossible task ahead of me finally put me over the edge.

Two of my classes asked me to go point by point through the
institute's special seminars and use the Bible to prove them true.
At first, I genuinely tried to complete the assignments, but I struggled to find verses that actually matched the things they claimed.

Eventually, as deadlines loomed and assignments piled up, I grabbed our trusty Strong's concordance—every godly family had one of these enormous, ten-pound books—and started searching. I looked up specific key-words, finding verses that I could tweak or write out just enough to make them sound right. Surprisingly, my online teacher never corrected me.

As I continued to use this method to prove the institute's points, I started to get suspicious. I wasn't finding anything genuine to back up the supposed truth. What if this was how it had all been proven originally? Ironically, the very education that was supposed to protect me from backsliding in a secular college environment planted the seeds of doubts that eventually freed me from my cultic beliefs.

Unfortunately, it's not just ultra-conservative Christians or religious cults that use the Bible out of context. I hear verses taken out of context all the time. Recently I was doing a popular women's Bible study with a group of friends. After we read a chunk of Scripture the author was using to make a point, we stopped and looked again. When we backed up and read the previous verses, it was obvious that the author hadn't considered context. Her point wasn't necessarily wrong, but it couldn't be backed up with this particular Scripture passage. Just because someone uses a Bible verse to prove a point doesn't make them right. If we are going to find the truth, it's vital that we understand what the Bible is and why it was written.

I realize that I am kind of hard-core on this topic, but being lied to for over a decade by someone who claimed to be getting truths from God's Word has made me sensitive. And it's not only me. I have seen well-meaning believers have their faith train wrecked when God didn't come through for them in the way they thought they'd been promised. I know of parents who prayed for healing a child with cancer. They had all the faith in the world, claimed promises out of Isaiah 53:5, "by his stripes we are healed," and 2 Corinthians 5:7, "for we walk by faith, not by sight," and their child still died (NKJV). Doubt and disillusionment nearly destroyed them. Reading the Bible and claiming promises out of context damages us and those around us because it gives us a false idea of God. We turn God into a vending machine and push certain buttons to make things happen. That's not the real God.

◼ | ◼ | ◼ | ◼ | ◼

When people of other religions become Christians, they leave behind their old religious books (e.g., the Koran or the Book of Mormon) and start reading the Bible. It seems obvious. But what if the religious book we need to leave is also the one we are supposed to read? How do we leave behind the Bible and then start reading the Bible? That sounds ridiculous.

For many of us who were hurt by some form of religious Christianity, this is what needs to happen. It's a complicated and confusing process that involves a lot of questions. How do we locate the truth when it's supposedly found in a book that was used to tell us lies? How do we unravel lies about the God of Christianity without leaving Christianity altogether? I'll be honest, sometimes we have to leave it all, for a while at least. If this is you, I want you to know that it's okay. Your questions and confusion are legitimate. They are difficult to face, let alone answer.

Unfortunately, the Bible can be used to say just about anything. Grab a verse here and a verse there, or half of a verse, and you can prove whatever you want. It's especially effective if you use a version with outdated English, one that's full of words no one uses anymore and definitions that have changed over the years.

Not only is this the wrong way to use the Bible, it's also spiritual abuse. Regrettably, this type of abuse is not uncommon within religious Christianity. People looking for power tend to abuse the Bible in order to control others. And then they wonder why people are leaving the church with a broken view of God and want nothing to do with His Word. The Bible calls itself a two-edged sword, but too often it's used like a club full of spikes.

As a teen and young adult, I was never taught how to correctly read the Bible. I never thought to consider the context of the verse and passage, the culture of the original audience, or the author's intent. Any verse could mean anything to anyone. As a result, it was easy for spiritual authorities to control those around them because they could make god say absolutely anything, and who were we to disagree?

We were told to look for *rhemas* as we read the Bible. I was taught that a rhema (in reality, the Greek word for *word*) was a verse or portion of Scripture that the Holy Spirit brings to our attention with application to a current situation or need for direction. We were supposed to use these words or phrases to guide our lives. It didn't matter if the word used in the King James Version had a different meaning than today, or if the verses were out of context, or if the prophecy was about the nation of Israel or even Jesus Himself. The Bible became like a religious Ouija board. We attempted to use God's Word to find specific answers to our questions, and then we claimed that they came from god. God told people to move to specific towns, leave their jobs, and marry off their children through this method. It sounds crazy now, but when spiritual leaders are claiming to have found hidden mysteries and secret revelations, their followers feel the pressure to find them too.

It makes total sense, after going through this kind of craziness, that people can't handle the Bible anymore. It was used to control and abuse them. How in the world can it be good or from God? It's way easier to completely reject something and find a new thing to believe. Seriously, how in the world are you supposed to find the truth when it's only a foot or an inch away from the lie?

I know I'm not the only one who either has or does struggle with the Bible. The book we call God's Word can seem so mysterious, so confusing and mystical. If this is you, I absolutely do not blame or condemn you. I get it. I do. But can I propose something? What if it's not the Bible that's the problem? What if it's the people who used it? What if the Bible was distorted and abused for their own benefit? What if the Bible you think you know is a lie?

I find that people who reject the Bible often reject it based on other people's opinions—things they have heard about it—and not on what they've read for themselves. If we could step back for a minute, even those of us who grew up in spiritually abusive Christianity would probably discover that we don't struggle with the Bible itself. We struggle with the voices in our heads as we read. We struggle with the things we were told by other people— the lies and the abuse we suffered.

Before I go any farther, I want you to know that I absolutely believe that the Bible is the infallible (foolproof, reliable, and watertight) and inspired Word of God. All of it. The Bible itself is not the problem. The problem is we don't understand how to read it. We don't understand what it really is or how to use it.

॥ ॥ ▄ ॥ ॥

I was out, graduated from secular college and married to my completely opposite husband, before I started to understand how the Bible was put together. We were at a tiny Bible college in the state of Wyoming, and my husband was taking a class on Biblical interpretation. One day we were talking about class and all of a sudden a light bulb turned on. "You mean, the books of the Bible have different purposes? They were written to different people? The prophecy books are mostly meant for the nation of Israel, and I can't apply them to whatever I want? Verses have specific interpretations, and they can't mean totally different things to different people? Understanding the culture of the day is im- portant?" My questions came hard and fast. The Bible had always seemed so mystical and mysterious, but it began to feel more concrete and understandable.

A few years later, our church small group went through Max Lucado's *The Story*. It took us chronologically through the Bible in thirty weeks. I know it sounds long, but it was incredible. For the first time, I saw the Bible for what it truly is: the story of God and the people He created. As we worked our way through the

Old Testament, and the stories and prophecies all intertwined according to when they were written, do you know what I saw? I saw Jesus. There were hints of the coming Savior from the very beginning. By the time we got to the New Testament, I was almost giddy with eager anticipation. And then, there He was, coming so unexpectedly, so humbly, showing us the heart of the Father. It was incredibly beautiful and moving. I got to see the big picture of God's plan for the world.

Unfortunately, this big picture is what we are often missing. You don't know how many Christians I run into who tell me that they really don't know anything about the Bible. Honestly, I don't know what is more concerning: Christians who don't know anything about the Bible, Christians who believe crazy things about the Bible, or Christians who are so burned by what people pretend the Bible says, that they can't even pick it up anymore. Guys, this is a problem! The truth about who God is, who we are, and what Jesus has done is found in the Bible. But too many of us don't know how to read it, use it, or what to believe about it. What if we could cut through the lies and junk and hurt surrounding the Bible and get a simple picture of what it really is?

Can I set some things straight, some of the lies Christians often believe? There is no *one inspired version* of the Bible. There are some beautiful translations and some wonderful paraphrases. Which one you choose to read should depend on where you are spiritually, how intellectual you want to be, and honestly, which you prefer. God is big enough to speak through any of them.

The Bible is an ancient book written thousands of years ago by people in a Middle Eastern civilization, and we read English translations as Western thinkers. There will be parts that we won't understand or get without studying. We should expect that. At the same time, it was written by everyday people for everyday people. Some passages may be more challenging than others, but today we have an amazing resource called The Internet. There are some wonderful websites such as Blue Letter Bible or the NET Bible that provide free Bible study resources. The more you read the Bible, the more familiar you will become with certain concepts or ideas. The Bible is really good at interpreting itself if you keep going and don't give up.

The Bible is not supposed to be a magic eight ball that gives us specific answers to specific problems. Sometimes God will speak to you through a verse or chapter, and it will be amazing. But we cannot open it at random and point to the page and expect that to be God's voice. The Bible has many purposes, but being our religious Ouija board is not one of them.

We can't cut up the Bible and take out parts we don't like or don't agree with. But that also doesn't mean that we accept someone else's opinion about those parts. We need to do a little personal digging—look into context, original audience, and author intent. Remember, logic and intellect aren't always the winners when it comes to God. And just because our secular culture believes something, doesn't always make it right. However, we don't need to obnoxiously smack people with our biblical beliefs either. We can believe the whole Bible and still treat people with love.

If these are lies about the Bible, then what is the truth? What is the Bible? The Bible is history—the story of God and the people He created. The Bible is prophecy—some of which has been fulfilled and some of which is still to come. The Bible predicts a Savior and then reveals Him to us. It shows us our value as God's creation and encourages us to seek after the God who made us. It demonstrates God's incredible grace, love, forgiveness, mercy, and faithfulness. But even more than this, the Bible claims that it is alive, powerful, and able to change hearts, all by itself. I've seen this happen.

During our first year of Bible school out in Wyoming, I taught math to sixth-to-twelfth-graders at a Catholic residential psychiatric treatment facility. It was quite the ten months. Almost immediately, I had some run-ins with a young self-proclaimed Satanist named Ben. He was a sweet kid and willing to dialogue about God, but he was also determined not to believe in Him. I bought him a book called *101 Reasons to Believe in God*. It contained a bunch of little proofs from science, psychology, the Bible, and more. All pretty gentle. Ben refused to read it. He even left it behind after he moved on from the facility.

However, his roommate Matt picked it up, was intrigued, and began to read. A while later, Matt came up to me after class and started talking about the book. He asked me if I could get him a Bible. *Um, yes!* I found him an easy-to-read translation and he was excited.

A few weeks later Matt told me that he had read Genesis and Ex-e-do-sis. Knowing Leviticus was next in line, I encouraged him to skip to the New Testament. We didn't talk again for a while.

Time went by. One day during after-school detention the kids in my room started talking about the saddest books they'd ever read. Matt piped up, "Luke. Luke was the saddest book I've ever read." I was surprised. He smiled. "But then I read it again, and I realized it wasn't sad after all."

I asked Matt if he liked Jesus. Of course he did. So I sent him to the book of John. A week or so later, Matt was back in my room telling me about Jesus and about how he believed in Jesus and that he knew Jesus had died for him. No one shared the Gospel with Matt. No one told him how to be saved, or preached to him, or led him in a prayer. Matt read the Bible, believed it, and met Jesus. This is the point. This is the purpose of the Bible.

When you take an honest look at your heart and your opinion of the Bible, what words come to mind? Mystical, difficult, boring, old-fashioned, and complicated? Or alive, amazing, revelatory, and life-giving? Are you willing to let God show you the truth about the book He wrote for us? Will you try to separate what people have told you about the Bible and what the Bible actually says?

I know that it might be super hard, but this is where we have to start. The Bible has been twisted and misused in order to abuse and control people throughout the centuries. But it's not the book itself that's the problem. It's the people who use and abuse it. Please stick with me as I share some of the lies I used to believe and the truths I have found about the amazing real God of the real Bible.

THE BIBLE CAN BE USED OUT OF CONTEXT TO CONTROL AND ABUSE PEOPLE. IT IS REALLY THE STORY OF GOD AND HIS PURSUIT OF THE PEOPLE HE CREATED.

WAYS OF SALVATION

Head down, Val hesitantly admitted how distant she felt from God—how distant she had always felt. Even though she had walked the aisle at church multiple times and given her life to the Lord on numerous occasions, she still felt disconnected. "It's like there is a blockage between us," she whispered with tears in her eyes, "and I can't figure out what it is."

···

"What must I do to be saved?" the Philippian jailer asked Paul and Silas in Acts 16. It's a good question, an important question. The most important question. But if you were to ask this question to a group of random Christians, you would probably get a variety of answers. You might hear things like: Pray the sinner's prayer. Ask Jesus into your heart. Raise your hand. Make Jesus the Lord of your life. Repent of your sins. Get baptized. Admit, Believe, and Confess (ABC). Receive the Holy Spirit.

How can there be so many ways to be saved? What is going on within Christianity that we can't even agree on this issue that is so fundamental to our faith? Would you know how to answer the jailer's question? Do you feel a little confused? It's okay. Although it's the pivotal point of the Christian religion, we tend to make salvation a bit complex.

If you look back at that list of answers, you might notice that all of them are *Christianese* again. If you were not already familiar with Christianity, most of these phrases wouldn't even make sense.

In a Philippian jail that had been recently rocked by a supernatural earthquake, a newly freed Paul and Silas looked at the shocked jailer standing in front of them. In fear and amazement, he asked a question and they answered. This is what they said.

"Believe in the Lord Jesus, and you will be saved" (Acts 16:31). Why do we complicate salvation? Can it really be this simple? Does it only take faith? Isn't that cheap salvation?

I think it's this simple. Faith is the key. And it's anything but cheap.

What if salvation isn't what we have been taught it is within our version of religious Christianity? What if we have missed the truth because of our obsession with behaviors? What if it is far deeper and more amazing than we could ever dream? What if it is less about perfection and more about abundant life? What if salvation is about restoration, recreation, and redemption? What if the "good behaviors" we often seek are a by-product of a genuine connection with the very real God of the universe?

As Christians we talk about the Gospel, but if we don't define that word, it can easily become more Christianese. The word *gospel* means "good news." We capitalize it and use *Gospel* to refer to the story of Jesus Christ's death and resurrection. Often Christians also include how to "get saved" within their Gospel presentation. But have you ever heard someone share the Gospel in a way that's anything but good news? I have.

There is the version that focuses on what terrible, horrible, no-good sinners we are. This version wants to convince people of the desperate wickedness of their hearts. It concentrates on God's wrath and how we all deserve hell. I listen to this Gospel presentation and I feel worthless and depressed. The god they talk about isn't someone I really want to spend time with anyway.

I've also heard a version of the Gospel that tries to guilt me into surrendering everything to Jesus in a desperate attempt to make Him Lord. I am left with a heavy load of *shoulds* piled high on my back. My eternal destiny is in question as I ponder whether I've really given up enough for Jesus. This god seems demanding and I'm not sure I'll ever measure up to his expectations.

These are two examples. There are many more Gospel versions that are not exactly good news. If you dig into these bad-news-gospels, you will probably find two things: something you need to do to appease God and a list of expected behaviors. Does this sound familiar? We just talked about it in chapter three. It's religion again. We are trying to do something to appease God. The real Jesus doesn't work that way. God doesn't need to be appeased because He has already appeased Himself.

❚ | ❚ ▄ ❚ | ▪

I don't remember my first exposure to the story of Jesus. But because my family was super involved in church, I'm sure I was quite young. We went to Sunday school, morning church, evening church, and Wednesday night church during my first twelve years of life. I loved church and my Sunday School, junior choir, and Whirlybirds class (sort of like AWANA). Somewhere in the middle all of this, I decided that I believed in Jesus and wanted to get baptized.

The church we attended during my childhood was the Church of Christ, and baptism is an essential part of salvation in that denomination. I was only seven years old when our pastor came over to the house to interview me and make sure I really believed the right things before I was baptized. I remember sitting with him at the dining room table. I felt old and important. I don't remember what we talked about, but apparently I passed because he allowed me to get baptized.

I chose a Wednesday night before junior choir because I didn't want the whole church to see me. But apparently getting ready took longer than I realized, because when my daddy brought me up out of the water, most of the junior choir and a few adults were there watching. I vividly remember the kids cheering and clapping. I felt new and clean. While I don't believe that baptism is what saves, I do know that this was a crucial moment in my life.

We attended the Church of Christ until I was thirteen. Every Sunday, instead of an altar call, they would do a baptismal call, inviting people to come forward and be baptized to demonstrate their trust in Jesus.

We then left the Church of Christ to join the crazy, cultic church that we were a part of for the next eight years. In name it was Baptist, but it was much closer to independent fundamental than mainstream. Each week we filled a rented hall with large homeschooling, ultra-conservative families who all followed the same man and organization.

At the church's peak, families were traveling up to two and a half hours to attend Sunday services, some even coming from Canada. There was no Sunday school, nursery, children's church, or youth group. Everyone sat through a long service, ate lunch together, and then sat through a second service. It was an all-day event. We sang hymns accompanied by a piano, listened to sermons, gave testimonies, and had men's prayer time where all the men filed forward to stand together awkwardly and pray in front of all the women and children.

At the time I was totally on board, trying to be one of the godly ones, and buying into the legalism hook, line, and sinker, so I didn't mind. It felt safe to be with people who were like me. The singing—complete with four-part harmony—was beautiful in that echoey old hall. The sermons were passionate and intense. I liked hearing testimonies about what God was doing in people's lives.

I really believe that our lead pastor meant well, and that he genuinely thought he was doing the right thing. However, when I look back, I can see all the craziness and brokenness caused by extreme legalism driven by behavior-based religion. But even more than that, one thing stands out as completely missing: the Gospel.

I don't remember ever hearing a Gospel message or an opportunity to get saved in any fashion. There were plenty of ways to appease god, ample things to do to get more blessings and make him happy, but we didn't really talk about Jesus.

While more mainstream, the next two churches in my life were still stereotypical Baptist complete with the NKJV Bible, no drums on stage, and a list of behavior expectations. They were each brief experiences about a year long and I don't have any clear memories of how the Gospel was presented. My next run-in with the good news of Jesus Christ happened at Grace Church in White Lake, Michigan.

Pastor Steve pulled me aside after my lesson to talk. I was passionate about working with the fifth- and sixth-graders and loved teaching them once a month. Although I was attending secular college, wearing pants, and listening to contemporary Christian music, my past was enmeshed within my heart. I'd never heard the phrase *lordship salvation* before Pastor Steve's little discipleship moment with me. It just made sense to my still-behavior-driven heart that if we were actually saved then we would surrender everything to God.

Pastor Steve talked to me about grace and salvation as a free gift. He explained that at this church they didn't do altar calls or ask people to pray a prayer—they focused on sharing the good news of Jesus. Rather than have people trust in a moment where they prayed, or raised their hand, or gave their life to God, the church wanted people to trust in Jesus and what He had done on the cross. I wasn't upset or embarrassed by this encounter because

Pastor Steve corrected me with such love and acceptance, but I was slightly mystified. It was something to take away and ponder.

Four years later I sat in Richard Seymour's personal evangelism class at Frontier School of the Bible, madly scribbling notes and listening with wide open eyes as this little, frail-looking old man shared the good news like I'd never heard it presented before. Sometime during that semester I found my friend Kate crying on a park bench with her husband. Raised in church and in a good Christian family, supposedly saved at a young age, Kate realized that she'd never really trusted in Jesus. Mr. Seymour said that this happened every year. Students came to Bible school because they wanted to follow God and while there realized that they had never actually been saved. How does this happen? Probably because well-meaning churches often share a behavior-driven, religious Gospel and miss the actual good news. As you read this next paragraph, listen to all the verbs.

The behavior-driven Gospel: You do bad things and that makes you a sinner. Sinners are separated from God and condemned to hell. Jesus came and died for our sins on the cross. If we pray and ask Jesus into our hearts, then He will forgive our sins and let us go live with Him in heaven when we die. If you are really saved, then you will do good things. These are the good things you should be doing . . .

I know it's a little exaggerated, but does it sound familiar? We call something like this the Gospel, and I guess it kind of is good news. But it's also incredibly behavior-based—our behavior and God's. And it's missing something vitally important: Connection within a relationship. I don't believe that church people are purposely misleading others. Well-intentioned, sincere Christians don't recognize the signs of man-made religion.

While we were living in the state of Wyoming, studying at Frontier School of the Bible, my husband and I got connected with Dare2Share, a Colorado-based ministry dedicated to teaching teens how to share the Gospel. During one of their youth conferences I heard the missing piece of the salvation puzzle for the first time. They shared a neat little acrostic to help the teens remember the basic points of the Gospel, and my heart gave a leap of excitement.

G: God created us to be with Him.
O: Our sin separated us from God.
S: Sin cannot be removed by good deeds.
P: Paying the price for sin, Jesus died and rose again.
E: Everyone who trusts in Him alone has eternal life.
L: Life with Jesus starts now and lasts forever.

When Paul and Silas answered the Philippian jailer's question, they told him to believe in Jesus, but they didn't stop there. Acts 16:32 says, "And they spoke the word of the Lord to him and to all who were in his house."

There is a beautiful story woven through all of Scripture. It's the story of God creating people to be like Him. He made us capable of having relationships with one another and with Him. And even though His creations chose—and continue to choose—to do things their own way and break that relationship, God has never stopped pursuing them. The Bible is the story of God making a way back to Himself, and Jesus is the very middle of that story.

We are more than our outward behaviors, and if salvation simply starts and ends there, then we've missed the point. People were created to be magnificent beings—made in God's own image—with the capacity for amazing good. Although sin has corrupted and mangled that magnificence, it's still hidden inside. There is gold in each of our hearts. Not only does salvation reconcile our relationship with the Creator God, but it also begins to restore our beautiful selves as the Holy Spirit does His mysterious work inside of us.

We are broken in far deeper ways than just our behaviors. Jesus confronted the outwardly good Pharisees about this all the time. We've been corrupted to the core, and deep self-centeredness discolors everything. But our restoration and reconciliation to God through the cross of Jesus also creates far more than good outward performance. Jesus is changing our hearts, our motivations, and our attitudes as we connect with Him in an experiential way. It's not just about something we believe in our heads. It's about Someone we know with our hearts.

Each one of us was made to know God. And we will never find fulfillment in anything other than a close, intimate relationship with Him. We were made to be connected to God. Sin separated us, but Jesus reconnects us if we choose to accept His gift of forgiveness.

There is nothing we can do to reconnect by ourselves. We are helpless. But God loves us so much that He chose to come and live quietly among us to show us who He really is. Knowing that we could never do enough to appease Him on our own, He chose to appease Himself by selflessly suffering and dying on the cross. Jesus did it all, everything that was necessary, to welcome all of humanity back into His Presence. When He cried out, "It is finished," He meant it. Salvation has been accomplished and the choice to receive God's love, forgiveness, and grace is up to us. That my friends, is amazingly good news!

I listened to my new friend, Val, as she shared her heart and her frustrations with Christianity and God. She wanted to be close to God, but it wasn't working. Even though she'd gone forward in church and given her life to God on multiple occasions, she still felt a block between her and Jesus. I pulled my chair closer and asked if I could share some verses with her.

We turned to John 3:16–18: "For God so loved the world that he gave his one and only Son, that whoever believes in him shall not perish but have eternal life. [A familiar verse.] For God did not send his Son into the world to condemn the world, but to save the world through him. *Whoever believes in him is not condemned,* but *whoever does not believe stands condemned already because they have not believed in the name of God's one and only Son"* (NIV, emphasis mine).

"What if you have always struggled to feel close to God because you never understood salvation?" I asked. "What if you were always trying to do something instead of believing in and accepting what Jesus has already done?

Val examined the verses in front of her. "Can it really be that easy?"

I smiled. "I think it is." She sighed and I could almost watch a weight fall off her shoulders. Then she smiled.

I'm not sure exact moments of salvation are really all that important. Sometimes salvation is more of a process than a moment and that's okay too. There doesn't have to be a special prayer, or action, or anything. It's about what Jesus did, not about what we do, anyway. But a couple of years later, Val mentioned that weekend as being the time when everything changed for her. The block was gone and she found herself truly connected to Jesus Christ.

THE GOSPEL IS SUPPOSED TO BE GOOD NEWS.
JESUS DID EVERYTHING NECESSARY TO RECONNECT US WITH HIMSELF.

PART TWO
EMBRACING QUESTIONS

GOD'S DISAPPOINTMENT

I followed the path at my favorite park with desperation in my heart. I needed to talk to Jesus right now. My goals were to confess my sin and "get right" with Him somehow so that all my problems would go away. In my mid-twenties and four years away from the cultic organization we'd followed, I looked pretty normal to the untrained eye. I was now wearing jeans, had cut my waist-length hair, was in a serious relationship with my boyfriend, and had almost finished my junior year at a secular college. But the legalism of my past was still entwined with my heart and mind.

While I may have perfected the art of looking good outwardly, on the inside I was a wreck. I'd always been the rule follower, the people pleaser, the *good* girl. I did the right things to make people and God happy with me. Although I didn't consider myself a perfectionist, being in control was very important to me. But I had totally lost that now. Worry and stress were consuming me. I was constantly fighting with anger and resentment. I had struggled with anxiety since childhood, but panic attacks were a new experience, and they were totally freaking me out. Since I had no clue what panic attacks were, but also didn't want to tell anyone,

I thought I might be dying. To top it all off, I felt overwhelmingly guilty for being so *out of control*. I knew that God must be horribly disappointed with me.

As I walked, confessed sin, and cried, I came to an opening in the woods. The trees thinned out, and sunbeams broke through the leaves in long, warm rays. A gentle breeze tickled my hair. I stopped. It was breathtakingly peaceful. As I stood there, it was like God put His arms around me. I felt His Presence and I could hear Him whisper to my heart, "I have never loved you more than I do right now."

My heart gave a jolt. I longed to believe that it was God speaking to me, but I doubted it because I had memorized Romans eight verse one. Because I grew up in a King-James-Version-only kind of environment (NKJV if you were edgy), the words streaming through my mind went like this: "There is therefore now no condemnation to those who are in Christ Jesus, *who do not walk according to the flesh, but according to the Spirit*" (NKJV, emphasis mine).

Maybe I had heard it in a sermon or maybe it was my own interpretation, but I always thought this Bible verse was saying something like this. If I was performing correctly, *in the spirit*, then there was no condemnation. However, if I was walking in sin, *in the flesh*, then I not only deserved but received condemnation.

I finished my walk filled with quiet confusion. After I got home, I grabbed my Bible and turned to Romans eight so that I could prove it wasn't really Jesus speaking to me. But the second half of the verse was missing. As part of my recovery process, I'd gotten a different Bible translation. My English Standard Version only said this: "There is therefore now no condemnation for those who are in Christ Jesus." What? That couldn't be right. I got out my laptop and started looking up various Bible translations to find the missing half of the verse. None of the other ones had it. There was no condemnation towards those who were in Christ Jesus. Period.

Could it be that Jesus not only loved me, but also *liked* me unconditionally? Somehow in my behavior-driven mind I had confused the two. Love seemed like something He had to do because He was God, but I was pretty sure He only liked me when I was performing correctly. My thought process kind of makes sense. Parents and teachers like us better when we follow the rules, and we feel their dislike when we are making poor choices. It can be hard to imagine God being different.

I slowly sank to the floor next to my bed in amazement. My mind was racing. I was in Christ Jesus. I had trusted Him as my Savior. I was His child; this was something I had never doubted. That meant that God did not condemn me. I sat there on the floor and let it sink in. He had never loved me more than He did right now, even though I felt like a complete and total failure. Tears rolled down my cheeks as I embraced this truth. I basked in it. I reveled. I let Jesus love me, and like me, even though it didn't make sense. He was so crazy, and amazing, and wonderful. It was my first glimpse of the beauty of God's scandalous grace.

The disappointment of God. I think it might even be worse than His anger. I don't know about you, but the fear that I have disappointed God pushes me down and away from Him. I feel overwhelmed by guilt and shame. How do I crawl my way back to a god who is sadly shaking his head at my failure?

What if God's disappointment is a lie? What if the real God doesn't ever get disappointed? What if it is impossible for Him to feel that emotion? Does that thought send a surge of hope through your heart? It's easy to imagine that God is like people around us, but God is not at all like us. He just made us to be a little bit like Him.

Does this sound too good to be true? Maybe even a little un-biblical? Are you worried that I'm making something up that feels good? I've searched the Bible trying to find God's disappointment and it's not there. While I found instances where God felt angry or sad about sin, I have never found Him disappointed. Why not? Because God cannot feel disappointment. Does that sound crazy? Keep reading.

Disappointment is a purely human emotion. To feel disappointment, you must have higher expectations for someone than they can, or choose, to meet. But God doesn't have higher expectations than we can meet. He knows everything about us, including the absolute depths of our brokenness, and He chooses to love us right there in the middle of it. Nothing surprises Him. He knows about the secret sin that we can't seem to get rid of. He knows about the anger and hurt we hold inside. He knows the things we hope no one else ever finds out. And even though He knows, He loves us, He forgives us, and He offers grace. The real God is not disappointed in us. He will never be disappointed.

Jesus told a story about two men, one a tax collector and the other a Pharisee. They both went to the temple to pray. The religiously righteous Pharisee stood in a noticeable spot and loudly announced all his good behaviors in a prayer. But the tax collector, a man who was considered a traitor and a sinner, stood at a distance from everyone else. Head bowed, eyes on the floor, he acknowledged his sin and begged for God's mercy. Jesus declared the broken tax collector justified before God. That's good news for you and me.

What if we could remove all guilt from our relationship with God? What if we didn't feel shame because we aren't being *spiritual* or haven't been *spiritual enough* lately? What if we could come to Jesus in freedom, despite what we have or haven't done, because we really believed in the forgiveness He has given us? What if we accepted and lived in God's unconditional love and grace? It might radically change our lives.

If you are a broken, messed-up sinner like I am, that is a surprisingly good thing. We are exactly the kind of people that Jesus hung out with when He was here on earth. Jesus didn't seek out the people who looked perfect on the outside. He didn't spend time with the religious elite. His closest friends were tax collectors and sinners—traitors and people who had no use for the Jewish law.

Did you know that? I did a little search on what the Pharisees meant when they called people *sinners*. It wasn't just a group of people who were behaving badly, it was most likely people who deliberately ignored Jewish laws and traditions. I find that incredibly fascinating.

Didn't God write the Mosaic Law? Why would Jesus choose to make traitors and intentional lawbreakers His closest friends? But He did. He welcomed these people, loved them, and ate meals with them. This acceptance and fellowship were some of the religious leaders' biggest complaints about Jesus. In fact, the Pharisees decided that He was guilty by association and condemned Him. They condemned God as a sinner; that's ironic.

Jesus declared that He came to seek and save the lost. He reminded everyone that sick people need a doctor and healthy people don't. He consistently broke religious and societal norms as He intentionally sought out lost and broken people. Jesus is incredible. I find Him absolutely compelling. Rarely do I struggle with feeling condemnation and disappointment from Him. The Old Testament God, on the other hand, is a different story. It might be hard to hate Jesus, unless you're an uber-religious leader, but the Jehovah of the Old Testament often has a bad reputation. This God does some pretty terrible things. He seems harsh and demanding. But is He really?

░ ░ ▄ ░ ░

I spent some time recently puttering around in the Old Testament during my coffee-and-Jesus time. Part way through Judges, I became confused. By the time I finished Ruth, and 1 Samuel, I was in shock. Half of the stories were missing. Or rather, the stories were there, but certain parts I remembered were gone. There were no morals, or explanations, or lessons. It was simply history. Stories of broken people and a God who connects with and uses them anyway.

Did you know God doesn't seem to care that Deborah is a woman in leadership? There is absolutely no negativity or suggestion that she is only leading because no good men are available—which I've heard most of my life. In fact, she is celebrated!

Struggling with fear and insecurity, Gideon needs not one but two signs from God before he obeys. God patiently provides miracles for Gideon without comment along with the strength to win an impossible battle. God does not appear fazed by Gideon's neediness or weaknesses. He never reprimands Gideon for a lack of faith.

Samson was basically a narcissistic, womanizing, self-centered jerk who only wanted revenge. There is no record of him ever repenting or caring about God at all. Even in the end, when God gave Samson back his strength, Samson only wanted it so that he could kill his enemies. Yet somehow Samson ends up in the hall of faith in Hebrews chapter eleven.

Do you know what hit me over and over again? The utter lack of condemnation. The Bible records stories in a historical, matter-of-fact way. God interacts with broken people to accomplish His purposes. Nothing stops Him. And the only condemnation was in the commentary. I actually had to stop reading the commentary in my study Bible because it was so irritating to me. If God's not condemning these people, we sure don't have any business adding it in. And yet we do. Well-meaning church people condemn the Old Testament characters in Sunday school, sermons, and devotionals. We humans can't seem to get away from an obsession with behaviors and a desire to moralize and judge. We insist on making sure people know that certain actions are bad. But is that really what's important?

The last five chapters of Judges record some historical events that happened before there was a king and *when everyone did what was right in their own eyes*. They aren't pretty stories. It's a dark time in the nation of Israel. Judges ends on that note. The tabernacle, the priesthood, and the worship of Jehovah have become twisted and corrupted. Everyone is doing whatever they want.

Next, the book of Ruth jumps back in time and tells the story of two women who lived during the book of Judges. Ruth was a

Moabite who followed her mother-in-law to Israel after her husband's death. She ends up marrying another Israelite man and
goes on to be the great-great-grandmother of King David's son
Solomon, the king who built the temple.

Why is this important? Well, in Deuteronomy 23:3, the Law
declares that no Moabite may enter the assembly of the Lord even
to the tenth generation. There are only four generations between
Ruth and Solomon. Only three generations are between a Moabite
and David, *the man after God's own heart*. And Ruth is in the line of
the Messiah—Jesus Christ. What is going on? What kind of ridiculous mercy and lavish grace is being shown by Jehovah? What
happened to the harsh, demanding god who wrote the Law?

Maybe he doesn't exist.

Maybe God isn't who we assume He is. I mean, who better
to disregard the Law than the One who wrote it? Maybe the Law
was never meant to be perfectly followed. Maybe it was only a
standard of perfection. Maybe the Law was meant to show us the
heart of God. In our broken obsession with behaviors too often
we've missed the point.

As I continued my journey through the Old Testament, I finally
arrived at 1 Samuel. It quickly became my favorite part. I had left
off chronologically at the end of Judges with terrible and tragic
situations in a time of spiritual darkness. But into that darkness
came the prophet Samuel.

Even though most of the country is a spiritual mess, Samuel's
parents Hannah and Elkanah seem to know the Lord personally.
I believe that God always has been, and always will be, found by
those who seek Him. After being given a miracle baby, Hannah
gives her young son back to God and sends him to live with the
priest Eli and serve in the tabernacle. Eli's sons are totally out of
control and yet are serving as priests. Worship at the tabernacle
has been corrupted by thievery and prostitution. But this doesn't
stop God.

In the beginning of chapter three we read that "the word of
the LORD was rare in those days; there was no frequent vision."

Yet, in chapter two, an unnamed man of God shows up out of nowhere and gives Eli a prophecy about his sons. Where did this guy come from? What is his story? I wish I knew. But God is still moving and working even though corporate worship is a mess.

And then, directly after the declaration that God is not speaking to people, He audibly calls the child Samuel. Verse seven of chapter three specifically says that at this point Samuel does not yet know God and has never had God's words revealed to him. All that is about to drastically change. Samuel will go on to become a mighty prophet of the Lord.

Into a time of spiritual darkness and depravity, Jehovah shows up. He calls people, speaks to people, and patiently reveals Himself to them. He isn't harsh, demanding, or condemning. They haven't been following the Law, but He doesn't even mention that. The God of the Old Testament is not who we think He is.

It's not that God doesn't point out sin, because He does. But He points it out in a matter-of-fact way, with abundant grace and truth, and with an utter lack of condemnation. There is no shame or judgment. His conviction is meant to draw people to Him not push them away. The more I read the Old Testament, the more Jehovah reminds me of Jesus. Wild, isn't it?

"He [Jesus] is the image of the invisible God, the firstborn of all creation" (Colossians 1:15).

What would it do to your relationship with God if you could believe that He and Jesus are the same? What would happen if you could truly accept that God is not disappointed in you? What if you were able to live without feeling God's condemnation? What if it was okay to be broken? What if you could freely bring that brokenness to God and allow Him to heal you? I think that would be amazing.

GOD IS FULL OF GRACE AND LOVE,
NOT CONDEMNATION AND DISAPPOINTMENT.

7

BROKEN HEARTS

"I'm using you as a safe space. I'm struggling in faith." I opened Facebook one afternoon to find this message from my online friend Kenzie. She continued, "My ex-fundamental atheist friend makes sense. My heart is heavy."

As I thought about how to respond, I was struck by how different my reply would have been a few years ago. I would have been much quicker to give advice and Bible verses. I would have felt panicked inside as I tried to convince Kenzie not to give up on her faith. But brokenness has a way of changing people. Going through our own times of garbage and mess tends to strip away our easy and automatic Christianese answers. It's painful, but it's ultimately a very good thing. So, this is what I wrote back:

You can be an atheist if that is where you need to go. And if Jesus is real, He will find you again. Sometimes the god we think is real needs to die so that the real God can exist. It's okay to wonder and question. It's actually really healthy. If God exists, He is big enough and loving enough to handle it. Thank you for trusting me with this information. I love you and am praying.

Have you ever had questions and doubts that you were terrified to admit? Maybe you did find the courage to admit them, only to be shut down or condemned. I know what it feels like to ask legitimate questions that need answers but are rejected instead. I know what it feels like to have people express their disappointment in you because they expected more from you as a Christian. It hurts. It's disillusioning. It makes you feel like curling up in your shell and hiding or maybe running far away. There is a level of desperation and loneliness that is hard to explain. But guess what? That's not the real Jesus.

The truth is that it's okay to be broken. It's okay to have questions and doubts. It's okay to reevaluate your faith. It's a good thing. In the last year I have had multiple friends come to me with some scarily honest confessions. They admitted things like *I'm not even sure what I believe these days. I think I'm losing faith. I don't even like going to church. I don't know how to be a Christian anymore.* While these can be frightening realizations to come to, I've also come to find them exciting.

I believe there is great value in losing our faith. There is significance in realizing that we don't know everything. There is beauty in the mystery of unanswered questions. Rather than something we should be afraid of, I think it's something to welcome. Too often religious Christianity delights in straight answers, cut-and-dried theology, and blind faith. There isn't room for doubt or questions—that's not healthy.

The real God is definitely big enough to handle our doubts, confusions, and questions. They do not scare Him. In fact, I think He loves them. Losing my faith, not once but multiple times, is one of the best things that's ever happened to me because of what happened next.

The first time I lost faith, I was in my early twenties. Life had drastically changed in the last couple of years. I'd left home to work as a live-in nanny while pursuing my degree in elementary education. Mary Poppins made being a nanny look easy, and I'll be the first to admit that my expectations for life were still rosy and naive. Reality was much harder. On top of my difficult nanny job, I was going through a year of intense personal change, both inside and out. I cut my waist-length hair and started wearing pants full time. While I was still attending a conservative Baptist church on Sundays and Wednesdays, on Thursdays I started going to a charismatic college group. They had wild worship music with drums and a smoke machine. Hanging out with normal people my age took some adjustment, but I loved it.

As nanny-hood lost its luster, I started looking for a new job. Somehow I got connected with a Christian group home for troubled boys. I started going there for prayer meetings and was fascinated. Having always loved working with broken kids, I was thrilled when a job opened up as a caregiver for the residents. Surely this was God giving me the desires of my heart and getting me out of my nanny job at the same time.

I applied and had an interview. It was amazing, and I was totally confident. God was so good to me. Then I didn't get the job. Looking back I can obviously see the red flags over a young, clueless, sheltered homeschooled girl working as a caregiver for delinquent teenage boys. What could go wrong? It makes me laugh just thinking about it. But at the time, I was so sure it was God. And then it wasn't.

About the same time, I got news that a young man I'd cared about for almost my entire life was continuing to make bad choices that would affect him forever. I had prayed for this guy for years and nothing ever happened. It seems like a little thing, but it was the straw that broke me.

▐ ▏▐ ▋▐ ▏▉

I sat at the black metal desk in my little room and stared at my open journal. I was still a nanny and I didn't want to be one anymore. I didn't get the job my heart longed for. My old friend was still choosing brokenness. Was God even real? Were my prayers being heard? Did He care? Was He truly good?

This was the first time I would ask these questions, but it wouldn't be the last. I've been at this place of lost faith more than once since then. Too often we think that struggle is a bad thing. But it's not. Wrestling is good. What if we chose to lean into the struggle and be fully present in that scary place of doubt and lost faith? What if we could believe that it was okay? That we are accepted, loved, and welcomed even with our doubts and confusion?

Christians through the centuries have faced seasons of doubt and what felt like a loss of faith. We often hear the phrase *a dark night of the soul* to describe this journey. A dark night was felt by the apostle Paul, C. S. Lewis, Mother Teresa, Martin Luther, Charles Spurgeon, and many others. Doubt is real, but it doesn't have the be the place where we stay.

Every season of doubt in my life has always led to increased faith and hope in a God that I can't let go of because He won't let go of me. The real God is bigger than our questions and doubts. He isn't mad at us for experiencing these things. He isn't disappointed. But God does want to redeem these places of brokenness. He wants to use them to shove our false gods off our god shelf. He wants to draw us to Himself.

It's okay if you are disillusioned with Christianity and the church right now. It's okay if you are questioning. Becoming disillusioned with our faith, feeling like we are losing it, is the first step to finding the real God for ourselves. Because He is real—He just might not be who we thought He was. The real God will never fit in the tiny places we want to keep Him. He is way too complex, enormous, and seemingly insane. I love that about Him. We will never understand Him. There will always be more of Him to experience and explore.

Unfortunately, there is a good chunk of modern Christianity that is empty tradition. It's the way we've always done it. God gets neatly wrapped in a package, and we forget that He is not tame or containable. Our god becomes more of a concept than a real and powerful Being. We get caught up in *doing* Christianity and we forget it's really about *knowing* and *being.* This is why I get excited when people tell me that they are losing faith. Because too often our faith is not actually in the real God; our faith is in the Christianese religion we were taught and the fake god we think we understand.

So let's struggle and wrestle, question and doubt. Let's go on a hunt for the real God. But as we journey, let's remember one thing. In real life there are more than two options; this complicated world isn't black and white. There are many answers to be discovered in the middle way. Truth is often found in tension, within two seemingly opposing realities. It's not less of a truth just because we can't totally wrap our minds around it. We are the creatures after all, and the Creator is the God of the universe.

❚ | ❚ ◼ ❚ | ◼

Maybe as you stare into the mirror, it's not a loss of faith you are experiencing but an overwhelming sense of your own brokenness. You feel hopeless because as hard as you try, you cannot get it together. It feels like you are running on a hamster wheel but are never really making progress. Looking around, everyone else seems to be doing this *good Christian* thing perfectly fine, but you are a failure. You are not alone in your feelings of hopelessness. The good news is that there are no good Christians.

We are all broken; some of us are just better at hiding it than others. We post cute things, or deep things, or whatever, on social media to try to make ourselves look like we have it together. We put on our plastic mask, our religious body paint, and maybe a little bit of spiritual glitter before going to church. But deep inside, many of us believe that if other people knew about our mess, then it would all be over.

Friends, if there is great value in losing our faith, then there is immeasurable worth in facing our brokenness. We will never be healed and never be free until we face our own mess. But we will never be able to face it while we continue to believe that God wants good people or that He somehow values our efforts at perfection.

The real God doesn't need us to appease Him because He already appeased Himself on the cross. And in the same way, the real God doesn't want our human efforts at perfection because He has already given us the absolute perfection of Jesus when we trusted in Him. We need to strive less and rest more. Hebrews chapter four, verses nine and ten, say, "So then, there remains a Sabbath rest for the people of God, for whoever has entered God's rest has also rested from his works as God did from his." What if we could believe this? What if we stopped trying to fix ourselves or get it together and instead gave it all to God and let Him fix it for us? What if we learned to rest in who He is and what He has done?

It can be terrifying to stare down our own brokenness, especially when we feel like God wants people to be good. But what if, as a pastor once said, "The greatest day of your life is the day you face yourself." How can this be? Let me share a paraphrased story from Luke chapter seven.

A Pharisee named Simon asked Jesus to have a meal at his house and Jesus went. People didn't sit in chairs at tall tables during biblical times like we do now; instead, they kind of reclined on pillows around a low table while they ate. The top parts of their body faced toward the table and their legs and feet stretched away from it. Hosts who wanted to appear generous often invited the poor, lame, and outcast to sit against the wall during the meal and later eat the leftovers. While Jesus ate, a woman sat against the wall. She wasn't just any woman; she was most likely a prostitute. This woman heard where Jesus was eating and purposely came into Simon's house to see Him.

She knelt by Jesus's feet weeping. In today's language, she was *ugly crying*. The tears poured down her cheeks and splashed onto Jesus's feet. She was a wreck, she was causing a scene, and she didn't care. As she cried, the woman let down her hair and used it to wipe away her tears and the dirt on Jesus's dusty feet. Then she kissed Jesus's feet and began to anoint them with precious ointment. This sinful woman was breaking all kinds of social norms and Jesus let her. In fact, I'm pretty sure He was smiling.

We don't have any idea what kind of interaction this woman and Jesus had earlier that day or week, but we do know that she loved Him. And we know that He loved her, accepted her, and forgave her. As the scene unfolded, the religious Pharisee started to freak out inside. "If this man were really a prophet, then he would know that this woman is an obvious sinner and he would never let her touch him."

But Jesus, knowing everything, including Simon's thoughts, told a story about two men who owed debts. One man owed a little money and the other owed much. When neither could pay, the moneylender canceled both debts. Jesus looked at Simon and asked, "Which man loved him more?"

Maybe Simon was starting to catch on to what Jesus was saying because he answered reluctantly, "I *suppose* the one who had a larger debt canceled."

"You're right," Jesus nodded. "People who are forgiven much, love much. But people who are forgiven little, only love a little."

If we are honest, it often feels easier to hide, cover up, and fake it. We feel guilty about being broken. We feel alone. Surely no one else is as screwed up as we are. We don't think anyone would understand. It doesn't help that the church often seems to say, "You are broken, so you'd better get it together. Fix yourself. Clean up your act. Or at least pretend."

Somehow within the Christian community we have created two categories of sins, *acceptable* and *unacceptable*. I'm sure that you can immediately think of sins to put in each category. But what happens when your sin is thrown in the unacceptable pile? We get good at hiding. And since we often feel like God is disappointed in us, we push Him away too. But we can never be healed until we dig through that brokenness and sin. We can never be whole until we realize that it's not about behaviors; instead, it's about the shattered state of our hearts. I don't know about you, but I want to be healed more than I want to pretend to be okay so I'm going to embrace the truth.

The whole world has been corrupted by sin, people included. We are all sinners. And each of us has empty, lonely parts that we try to satisfy in unhealthy ways. Maybe you struggle with anxiety, depression, an eating disorder, anger, gossip, a porn addiction, cutting, or something else. I struggle too. You are not alone. And underneath all those outward problems, it only gets worse because we are absolutely filled with self-centeredness. The very motives of our hearts are corrupted. We are all broken. We are terminal, and there is only one solution. Jesus. We need the real Jesus.

We need the God who let prostitutes wash His feet, rescued an adulteress from being stoned, chose traitors to be His followers, and said that He came to seek and save the lost. We need the Jesus who was holding children one minute and tearing up religious traditions with a whip the next. We need the One who says He is the exact image of the invisible God to bring us into the presence of His Father and heal us. And He will.

Contrary to the lies in our heads, our mess doesn't shock God. He already knows. We just need to come with our brokenness, like the prostitute, and lay it all at His feet. The real God doesn't expect us to fix ourselves; He knows it is impossible. Jesus wants to restore us, but we have to let Him.

What if we decided to be real and honest: honest with ourselves, with God, and with each other? What if we took our mess out of the closet and out from under the bed where we've been hiding it? What if we chose to believe the tension theology that we are totally broken and yet unconditionally loved? What if we allowed the cross of Jesus Christ to cover all of our sins? What if we realized just how much we have been forgiven? I think that we would discover freedom, peace, transformation, and the life that is truly life (1 Timothy 6:19 NIV).

WE ARE MORE BROKEN THAN WE KNOW,
BUT MORE LOVED THAN WE CAN EVER IMAGINE.

8

TRUE FREEDOM

The dirt road softly crunched under the tires of my red Ford Probe. I was a couple of hours early even though I had gotten lost. Turning the final corner, I got my first look at the place I would call home for the summer. There was an open grassy field, a cluster of cement-block cabins painted army barracks beige, an old farmhouse, and some tall trees. It wasn't much to look at. But although I didn't know it then, this humble little summer camp would change my life.

With nervous excitement, I pulled past the welcome sign and up to what I hoped was the office. I had never spent this much time with "normal" people before, people we used to call *worldly Christians*. Gathering my long, denim skirt, I slid out of the driver's seat and made my way up the hill to the office door. When I interviewed over the phone, I specifically asked the camp director if I'd be allowed to wear skirts all summer. There was a short pause, and then he replied that it would be fine as long as they didn't interfere with my work. I enthusiastically assured him that they wouldn't.

Since I was two hours early, I helped set up the old staff lounge for our week of training. I look back with a smile and a shake of my head, wondering what they must have thought of me. I came to camp thinking I was there to share Jesus with children. I had no idea that I would find freedom, grace, and "normal" people who not only passionately loved God but also willingly accepted me—ultra-conservative quirks and all.

What happened between that first day of staff training, when I arrived in my denim skirt, and the last day of camp, when I got a matching cartilage piercing with a new friend? I found freedom. It was a wild summer filled to the brim with brand-new experiences. Although I was disillusioned with legalism and starting to realize I may have been brainwashed, I still brought a suitcase filled with black-and-white beliefs to camp. But amid the silly skits, late-night laughter, inside jokes, and new friendships, I discovered the mesmerizing world of gray.

As I realized that God wasn't waiting for me to perform before He blessed me, I let go of silly rules. I clapped and swayed to contemporary praise music and experienced a worship that I didn't know existed. Believing in people's acceptance of me, I let my crazy side come out—participating in skits and planning pranks. Boys became my friends as we hung out, talked, and flirted. I even bought a couple pairs of loose capris. It was a beautiful, life-changing summer.

◾ ◾ ◾ ◾ ◾

We conveniently never studied the book of Galatians in my Christian cult. It is all about freedom from religious behaviors. The apostle Paul wrote Galatians to a church who began understanding grace but then got sucked into believing that they needed the law plus Jesus. A former Pharisee himself, Paul knew firsthand what life is like bound by rules. His passionate heart is clear as he opened in chapter one with "I am astonished that you are so quickly deserting him who called you in the grace of Christ." He called them foolish and said they had been bewitched in chapter three. And finally in chapter five, Paul declared that "It is for freedom that Christ has set us free. Stand firm, then, and do not let yourselves be burdened again by a yoke of slavery" (NIV).

What is real freedom? What does it look like? What does it mean to be free? Can we define it? Can freedom be about behaviors and not be about behaviors at the same time?

By the time I got to that little summer camp as a twenty-one-year-old adolescent, I was already halfway to freedom. Two things had happened that began the freedom process in my heart: I had met Jesus for myself, and I had begun to grasp the power of the Holy Spirit. I was already beginning to understand that my heart was what mattered. Rather than believing they earned God's approval of me, most of my standards were about trying to be different from the world. As I recognized that these rules didn't matter after all, they were easier to let go.

Standing in front of the mirror, I pushed back the long hair over my left ear and looked at my new cartilage piercing. It was a bold but necessary step. I was terrified and excited at the same time. I never wanted to forget the things I'd learned that summer. I wanted a visual sign that I was free every time I looked at the mirror.

Prior to my summer at camp, I judged anyone with extra piercings. Even double piercings in earlobes were suspect, because the only *godly* piercings were one set of small studs or tiny hoops worn in female ears. Anything more than that and you obviously didn't care about being holy. Looking at my beautiful new piercing, I couldn't help but smile. I knew that I loved Jesus and wanted to follow Him, *and* I now had an earring in the top of my ear.

It's easy to look at my extreme story of rules and behaviors and feel relatively free yourself. But it's worth a double check.

It's possible to exhibit behaviors that look free but are still legal-
istically religious. We can even be legalistic liberals. Remember,
as broken humans, we are naturally religious. We are naturally
focused on behaviors.

So, is freedom just doing things that we once believed were
wrong? Ironically, no. In fact, I know people who have tattoos,
drink craft beer, listen to secular music, and wear whatever they
want, but they are still completely shackled by legalism. They are
some of the most unfree people I've ever met. How is that possible?

True freedom starts in our hearts. It starts with questions we
must ask ourselves. Who is God? What does He want from me? How
does He feel about me? How do I feel about Him? What am I trying
to get from Him? What are the motives behind my behaviors?

Many Christians will tell you that they aren't legalistic—
even though they are following a specific code of behavior—
because they aren't trying to earn their way to heaven. However,
when we dig deeper, we will discover that they are still trying
to earn something: blessings, God's pleasure, people's positive
opinions, or maybe the image of a good Christian or a progressive
Christian. If we are trying to get something because of our behaviors, it's religion again. True freedom comes from a heart that
understands God's love and grace and is responding with love
in return.

I love change. I love freedom and nonconformity. But we
cannot confuse reaction with actual freedom that comes through
grace. It's strange, but reaction and freedom often look the same
outwardly. There might be changes in music, clothing, beliefs, or
education choices. People get tattoos and piercings. Sometimes
people start dating for the first time, dye their hair, grow dreads,
go to college, change jobs, or make other big life decisions. So,
how do we know if we are really free and not reacting to old rules
and expectations?

When we are motivated by reaction against legalism, old
standards, and religion, I think it looks a bit like this: anger
and frustration drive our choices, and these choices are often

a response to previous rules. If someone were to ask us why we do things, our answer would probably sound like, "Because I can, dang it. I'm free." But we don't feel very free. We feel stressed and tired because we are still *trying* to *do* something. We might be more consumed with things we *can* do instead of things we *shouldn't* do, but our focus is still on outward actions. And, because we are still obsessed with behaviors, deep down we also probably still struggle to believe that God actually loves us and wants a relationship with us.

I believe real freedom starts with understanding that our relationship with God has nothing to do with our own efforts and everything to do with Jesus Christ. Jesus came to show and give us grace, something we could never earn and would never deserve. The point of Jesus's death and resurrection was never to make us into moral people who followed the rules. God didn't save us to make us good. The point was to restore our relationship with the God who created us and loves us. He forgave us so that we could know Him. God wants to know us. We are free to be friends with Jesus. Knowing Jesus changes us, but the real change starts at the core of who we are and works its way outward. It is first about heart change and then about behaviors.

When we are free because we understand grace, our actions might look similar to someone still stuck in reaction, but our hearts are different. We might still get a tattoo or cartilage piercing, for example, but our motives are different. The reasoning is no longer "Because I can, dang it," but simply, "Because I want to." We aren't reacting to anything; we are resting in our relationship with Jesus. We are believing in the scandalous grace of God and extending that grace to others. Instead of obsessing over outward actions, our focus is inward on heart motivations. As we get closer to Jesus, we realize He is making us more like Him. His Holy Spirit is giving us things like love, joy, and peace. Because our heart is changing, our outward actions might change too. But that change is a result of God's beautiful grace and not an angry reaction to religion.

A few years ago, I was leading a college small group. One of the girls in my group initially joined us because she was facing the consequences of some bad decisions and had to temporarily move back in with her parents. The Holy Spirit caught her over the next few months and began to work in her heart. I'll never forget the day she came up to me with a puzzled look on her face. "I don't want to do the things I used to want to do anymore," she said. "And instead I want to do other things—new and good things." I laughed with her. This is the transforming power of God's grace.

Which is exactly where Paul ends up in Galatians chapter five. After reminding the church at Galatia that Jesus came to set them free from the rules of the law, Paul starts to talk about the work of the Spirit in our hearts: "But I say, walk by the Spirit, and you will not gratify the desires of the flesh . . . But if you are led by the Spirit, you are not under the law" (Galatians 5:16, 18). Paul lists the sinful works of the flesh and then the familiar fruits of the Spirit. "But the fruit of the Spirit is love, joy, peace, patience, kindness, goodness, faithfulness, gentleness, self-control; against such things there is no law" (Galatians 5:22–23).

When we are living a life that is surrendered to and satisfied in the real Jesus, we will find true freedom. We will still be broken, but we will also be whole because of Him. It will be less about behaving correctly or rejecting rules, and more about living from a heart that loves God, ourselves, and the people around us.

The world became far less black and white to me during those ten crazy weeks of summer camp. I began to recognize that just because I believed something was true didn't necessarily mean it was true. I discovered that it was okay to be wrong. My safe but rigid walls of right and wrong started to crumble. Living in the misty world of gray became more comfortable.

Life is complicated. People are complex. And the real God is insanely incomprehensible. We don't need to have all the answers;

we can embrace the mystery and paradox that exists. We can struggle, and learn, and process. We can change our minds. We can be wrong. This is the beautiful world of gray. This is the dwelling place of true freedom.

REAL FREEDOM IS MORE THAN BEHAVIORS;
IT STARTS IN OUR HEARTS.

9

SPIRITUAL FORMULAS

Looking at the ultrasound monitor, I didn't need anyone to tell me. I knew as soon as I saw him. My baby was dead.

I stared at my young husband in numb disbelief. He gently took my hand. Four weeks ago, our baby was wiggling all over that monitor, waving to us, measuring on track, looking good. But now he was gone. Why would God do this to us again?

We had lost our first baby seven months ago. I was sixteen weeks along on our first wedding anniversary and we celebrated my growing belly. But then at eighteen weeks, I had a miscarriage. Until now, it had been the hardest thing I'd ever gone through. We asked so many questions, felt so much grief, and yet learned so much as God carried us through.

Less than thirty minutes after the ultrasound my husband and I sat close together in a secluded waiting room. The dim lighting and multiple Kleenex boxes suggested that most people who sat there held similar broken hearts. We had been so careful with this pregnancy. There had been many more ultrasounds, and things had been looking good. It seemed like God was answering our prayers. But now our hearts were shattered all over again.

My mind filled with unanswered questions. Why would God let this happen? And what had we done wrong?

The doctor finally came. In a soft voice he told me our baby was bigger this time. He told me it would be better if I delivered him. He wanted to know if tomorrow would work. Tomorrow was Valentine's Day.

Valentine's Day will never be the same for me. Even after more than a decade, there is still a twinge. I spent February 14, 2009, in the hospital laboring with my tiny baby. It was a bit surreal. To be on the maternity floor. To hear babies crying. It lasted all day until finally, at 9:34 p.m., we got to hold our teeny, little baby boy. He was about fifteen weeks along (even though I was at seventeen weeks), with tiny fingers and toes, and little ribs. You could even see his fingernails starting to form. The nurses let us spend as much time as we wanted with him. It's hard to explain the pain I felt, kind of like my chest was ripping in two. I wanted that baby. I wanted him so much! But I wanted him to be alive, and he wasn't.

▌▐▐▟▐▌▐

Losing my two babies rocked my world. It shook my faith and exposed the formulaic way I was still thinking. I'd rejected much of the legalistic and religious ideas I'd learned as a teen in my Christian cult. But when I thought about my babies dying, I never remembered the fact that I had a deformed uterus—which was true. I only ever wondered what I had done wrong. I racked my brain for the lesson God was trying to teach us. I wondered if my husband or I were being punished for something. I wanted an A + B = C answer.

I'm guessing you can relate to this, maybe more than you want to admit. It's easy to say we believe that God is all-powerful and that He has the ability to intervene on our behalf. And it feels like our faith is working when life is going well and God answers our prayers with a yes. But what about when He doesn't?

What about when a young missionary couple loses their healthy newborn son to unforeseen complications after two previous miscarriages? When a wonderful, loving pastor's wife suddenly dies with no warning? When a Christian family battling cancer with their teenage son finds out their second son also has cancer? Really, God? If You are really in control and absolutely powerful, why would these things happen? We want an answer. We long for an explanation that makes sense.

There are plenty of examples of miracles in the Bible, and we've heard modern-day stories of miracles too. The outcome we want is good, and we know that God *could* do it. Our desires are possible. But how do we get God to agree? What will make Him cooperate? Can we twist His arm? Which combination of buttons do we push on His heavenly vending machine?

Wait, you don't talk like that? Me neither, at least not out loud. But that's often the secret dialogue in my heart. And I know I'm not alone.

Do you know what sells in the Christian marketplace? Formulas. An amazing number of books have been written that promise certain outcomes if we follow specific steps. There are many leaders within Christianity that preach formulas, steps, and promises, and they gather large audiences.

I've read formulaic thinking on blogs, and in books, and heard it from the mouths of Christians across the spectrum of theology. I have heard people take Bible stories and turn them into formulas. "Such-and-such Bible character did x, y, and got z, therefore, if we also do x, and y, we will get our z." Those books and speakers are popular because as broken people, we desperately want a way to be able to control this crazy world.

I was raised under the shadow of the King of Formulas. Our cult leader created steps for everything. Follow these three steps, or do those five steps, and you will get guaranteed blessings and success. A perfect example is a book he often recommended called *The Power of Crying Out*. The author basically compiled verses (mostly out of context) where people *called out* or *cried out*.

Then he turned around and promised that if we pray loudly, God hears us and will respond better than if we pray quietly. Because that makes sense. I'm being sarcastic. But if I was desperate for an answer, I might buy into it.

If following the right steps doesn't work for us, we might turn to claiming promises as the next formula in our bag of tricks. Have you ever heard this verse from Isaiah fifty-three used as a promise for physical healing? "By His stripes we are healed" (v. 5 NKJV). It's a pretty popular verse for healing, but there is a big problem with context. First of all, it's not even a whole verse; it's a phrase at the end of one. If we read the whole verse, the actual context is clear.

"But he was pierced for our transgressions, he was crushed for our iniquities; the punishment that brought us peace was on him, and by his wounds we are healed" (Isaiah 53:5 NIV).

We don't have to have a Bible degree to see that this verse is a prophecy about the coming Savior and how we would be rescued by his death. Jesus's wounds healed us, but it wasn't a physical healing, it was a spiritual one.

Here is another promise: "We walk by faith, not by sight." People use this verse to claim all kinds of things. But, as I've said before, we cannot rip verses out of the Bible and make them mean whatever we want. This phrase comes from 2 Corinthians five, ironically a chapter about heaven and one day being with Christ. It is not talking about getting healed physically. Here is verse seven, sandwiched between verses six and eight for context's sake.

"Therefore we are always confident and know that as long as we are at home in the body we are away from the Lord. For we live by faith, not by sight. We are confident, I say, and would prefer to be away from the body and at home with the Lord" (NIV).

Claiming promises like these—even if they were in context— is still at its root a formulaic approach. We are still trying to find a way to guarantee a specific outcome, force God's hand, and push the right buttons on God's vending machine.

If steps and promises don't work, the last formulaic response is often taking or pushing the blame. Have you ever heard or thought things like this? I guess I/they/we didn't have enough faith. As though there is a specific quantity of faith that requires God to act on our behalf in the way we want.

These are all real responses that I have heard from people when their prayers weren't answered the way they hoped. Somehow I doubt there is a specific amount of faith that will manipulate God into giving us what we want. Where do people get this idea that their lack of faith is to blame? From the Bible, unfortunately. There are tons of verses talking about having faith, and asking for things in faith. Here are two of them.

"He replied, 'If you have faith as small as a mustard seed, you can say to this mulberry tree, "Be uprooted and planted in the sea," and it will obey you'" (Luke 17:6 NIV).

"But when you ask, you must believe and not doubt, because the one who doubts is like a wave of the sea, blown and tossed by the wind. That person should not expect to receive anything from the Lord" (James 1:6–7 NIV).

If these were the only verses I read, then I could easily believe that I am at fault because of my lack of faith. However, when I take another look, I realize that Jesus is responding to His disciples' request for more faith. And their desire for faith is in direct response to a statement He made on forgiveness. We can't claim this verse as a blanket promise across the board. When I look closer at the James passage, I see in verse five that James is talking about asking God for wisdom. The specific promise is that if we ask for wisdom, God will give it to us. Unfortunately, there are no verses, used in context, that guarantee any and every outcome we desire based on our amount of faith.

Do you know what doesn't actually work in real life? Formulas. The real God is not a vending machine. We cannot enter A5 and B10 and get a Snickers bar and bag of Doritos every time. There is no way to gain control over this world full of hurt and disappointment. There is simply a very real Being who wants to walk through it with us.

∎ ∣ ∎ ∎ ∣ ∎

Sitting in the hospital bed, grieving my tiny baby, I was surprised when a nurse came in and asked if we had a name for him. I didn't have any names for dead babies, only living ones. We didn't know what to do. My husband and I were struggling to trust God and believe in His goodness. It felt impossible to hold on to hope. So after talking it over for a while, we chose to take a step of faith. We named our little son Trust. Not because we felt it, but because we didn't. We chose to trust in a God that we could not see and did not understand. And instantly, I felt peace flood my heart.

I know from experience what it means in Philippians 4:7: "And the peace of God, which surpasses all understanding, will guard your hearts and your minds in Christ Jesus." Because the peace I felt didn't make any sense. Nothing had changed in my circumstances, but I was suddenly filled with absolute peace. I knew with confidence that God was still in control.

I found Isaiah 45:6–7 before my babies died, but afterward it became my life passage. I had heard well-meaning people tell others who were grieving that God was sorry their pain happened. I didn't want God to be sorry, because I didn't want Him to be weak. I didn't want to imagine Him saying, "Oops, sorry about that." I wanted a God who was absolutely and completely in control.

"I am the LORD, and there is no other. I form light and create darkness; I make well-being and create calamity; I am the LORD, who does all these things" (Isaiah 45:6–7).

As I clung to this verse in Isaiah, I heard the Holy Spirit whisper to my heart, "Christy, I *took* your babies. I did it on purpose. It was not an accident." That knowledge gave me immense comfort. I felt safe in the arms of a God who was completely in control and loved me even if I didn't know what He was doing or why.

As I grieved with Jesus, I knew that I was intensely loved. I knew that we hadn't done anything to make this happen. I was confident that God in His infinite wisdom had done this on purpose, but that being so much bigger than me, He didn't owe me an explanation. And with that knowledge I was able to rest.

We were over one thousand miles away from family at a Bible school while these miscarriages were happening. I was alone and surrounded by other young couples, pregnancies, and babies, but in this place of deep loss and heartache, Jesus carried me. Through friends' pregnancies and baby showers, Walmart trips surrounded by teen mothers, and youth group with the teens who knew my story, God held me close. I cried often, but my tears were not tears of hopelessness and despair, just of sorrow and, somehow, a strange trust. Choosing to trust without formulas does not mean that we don't feel pain.

Amazingly, only one year after we lost Trust, despite thinking we might never have children, God miraculously provided a diagnosis, a fertility specialist who happened to be one of the best in the nation, eight thousand dollars in cash, a surgery, and a brand-new baby growing in my tummy. Sometimes God gives us the desires of our hearts even when it seems impossible. And other times He doesn't. And He doesn't always give us explanations for His reasoning.

My story had a happy ending, but I know people whose stories didn't. People who are still living with pain, loss, and unanswered questions. That's where the disconnect often comes in. How do we reconcile a supposedly good, all-powerful God with the good things that He fails to accomplish? This paradox is something I still wrestle with today. I wonder if our discomfort with paradox and mystery is what makes formulas so attractive. Perhaps we create religious formulas because we are trying to grasp a feeling of control in a shaky, frightening, and often heartbreaking world. We are trying to make sense of things we don't understand.

If there are no secret keys, no hidden formulas, no special chants, no magical ways to get God to do our bidding, then what can we expect? What has God truly promised us? The answer might surprise you.

"I have told you these things, so that in me you may have peace. In this world *you will have trouble*. But take heart! I have overcome the world" (John 16:33 NIV, emphasis mine).

"No temptation has overtaken you except what is common to mankind. And God is faithful; he will not let you be tempted beyond what you can bear. But *when you are tempted*, he will also provide a way out so that you can endure it" (1 Corinthians 10:13 NIV, emphasis mine).

"Remember what I told you: 'A servant is not greater than his master.' If they persecuted me, *they will persecute you* also. If they obeyed my teaching, they will obey yours also. They will treat you this way because of my name, for they do not know the one who sent me" (John 15:20–21 NIV, emphasis mine).

Wait a minute, we've been promised trouble, temptation, and persecution? That doesn't sound like a very nice promise. Isn't life with Jesus supposed to be warm fuzzies, roses, and sunsets? Isn't Jesus supposed to make our life better? Easy and peaceful? You might hear some people say that, but it's not exactly in the Bible.

The Bible very clearly tells us that the world we live in is broken. It happened at the fall when sin first came into God's perfect universe. Creation is broken, so we have things like disease and natural disasters. People are broken, so they make choices that hurt not only themselves but also those around them. This world will always be full of trouble but look at the other promises in those verses.

Jesus wants to give us peace. He encourages us by reminding us that He has overcome this world. He is faithful; He will provide a way out of the temptation. Jesus tells His disciples in John fourteen that He will not leave them alone; He is sending the Helper, the Holy Spirit.

The real God will not always make sense. So we've got to throw away the understandable, controllable god that we have created in our own image. We must allow the real God to be bigger, greater, and *more* than we can comprehend. Does the Bible say that God is good? Yes. All-powerful? Absolutely. Does He still choose to let bad things happen and take good things away? Yeah, actually the Bible says that too. And with that, we are back to tension theology—the opportunity to believe in two seemingly opposing things. In one hand I will believe in God's goodness and love, and in the other hand I will believe in His sovereignty even in a broken world.

Life is going to hurt, but we will never be alone. And a God who is more, better, and bigger than we can ever imagine is in complete control even when it doesn't look like it. He wants to walk with us through life, to help and comfort us, because He loves us. He wants to walk so close with us that He lives inside of us. "Do you not know that you are God's temple and that God's Spirit dwells in you?" (1 Corinthians 3:16).

That truth is so much better than a vending machine, or magic formula guaranteed to bring us what we want. God is a real, living, incredible, loving Being who wants us. He wants to be friends with us and help us. He wants to give us peace and joy despite the brokenness of this world, and not based on anything we do or don't do, but simply because of His amazing grace.

THERE ARE NO MAGIC FORMULAS,
BUT THERE IS A GOD WHO PROMISES WE WILL NEVER WALK ALONE.

10

HEALTHY FEAR

One of the most terrifying experiences of my teenage years was attending drivers' training. I wasn't scared of driving a car like you might imagine. Instead, I was afraid of going into the dangerous and wicked public high school. I'd heard whispered stories about the rampant evil that went on in that place every day. Although we drove by every time we went into town, I'd never actually stepped foot inside. The first day my parents dropped me off I approached the ominous front doors with a lump in my throat the size of a bowling ball.

Sitting in a desk for the first time in my life, I cast quick side-long glances at my classmates. I was the only one wearing a skirt and that fact only amplified my feelings of insecurity and isolation. A fish out of water doesn't even begin to describe how I felt. I was more like an alien who had landed on a strange and dangerous new planet and wasn't even sure she could breathe.

I would have felt more at home if someone had handed me a sunbonnet and told me we were going to learn to drive a covered wagon. I identified with Anne of Green Gables, Laura Ingalls Wilder, or any number of characters from the 1800s far better than my peers in the mid-1990s. Drivers' training was a stretch, but I survived, even if I did get asked if I was Amish.

Our organization used fear to separate and isolate us. I grew up afraid of the world I lived in. The only safe people were also part of our group. I was afraid of worldly people, modern culture, breaking the rules, and ultimately God Himself. Fear stopped questions and kept us from thinking for ourselves.

Fear is an excellent motivator if you want power. Capitalize on people's fears, convince them you have the only answer, and they will give you control. I see this same concept in many areas of our modern life. People often make choices about things like schooling, health, and politics based on fear. It might not be obvious on the surface, but if you look closely, you will see familiar underlying motivations. Social media, blogs, and the internet in general are all excellent ways to spread fear. You don't have to look very far to find scams and fake stories that went viral because of people's fear.

People in power like to use fear because it works. I know that personally. Which is partly why, as I began to get to know the real Jesus for myself, the things I had been taught began to make less and less sense. Jesus doesn't use fear to motivate people.

Fear is not from the real God. He is not a God of fear. He doesn't use fear to control us. These are important truths to grasp in our minds and believe in our hearts. I know that I am not the only one who has struggled with an unhealthy fear of God. Whether that fear came from leaders who incorrectly portrayed God's expectations and wrath, or from our own anxiety-ridden hearts, it's easy to believe that our performance determines how God feels about us. It's easy to go back to a formulaic way of thinking about the brokenness in this world. If we do this and that, then God will give us the blessings we desire. But if we mess up, then He is going to punish us. The real God doesn't work like that.

Did you know that there are over one hundred verses in the Bible telling us not to be afraid? Many of those intertwine a lack

of fear with the truth that God is on our side. Here are some of
my favorites:

"It is the LORD who goes before you. He will be with you; he
will not leave you or forsake you. Do not fear or be dismayed"
(Deuteronomy 31:8).

"In God I trust; I shall not be afraid. What can man do to me?"
(Psalm 56:11).

"But immediately Jesus spoke to them, saying, 'Take heart; it
is I. Do not be afraid" (Matthew 14:27).

"Peace I leave with you; my peace I give to you. Not as the world
gives do I give to you. Let not your hearts be troubled, neither let
them be afraid" (John 14:27).

For a long time, *the fear of God* was one of the most triggering
phrases for me in normal Christianity. It conjured up memories
of sitting in seminars, balancing a large red notebook on my lap,
and frantically filling in blanks while a little man on stage flipped
tabs on an overhead projector. Anecdotal stories assured us that
if we made the wrong decision or stepped out from under the
umbrella of protection, god would quickly zap us with punishment. Even the simple choice of which toothbrush to buy was not
without importance according to "true stories" shared to make
a point. Life was scary because god was scary. But not to worry,
our faithful leader could tell us exactly which steps to follow and
what standards to embrace so that god would bless us instead.
These initial seminars were followed by others in our organization, and together with a homeschool curriculum, they created
a worldview motivated by fear. At least that's how it felt in my
teenage mind.

I definitely grew up with a fear of God, but it wasn't a healthy
one. I felt afraid of god's wrath, sure that if I didn't perform
correctly or follow the right steps, he would punish me. The god
I learned about seemed distant, angry, and scary. Our leaders

focused on the Old Testament and its many laws. They created morals in familiar Bible stories, showing that people who didn't follow the rules got disciplined. They completely missed the mercy and grace that also fills those same stories.

My husband and I got to spend ten days in Israel a couple of years ago. I was intrigued by the religious Jewish community that lives in the Old City of Jerusalem. I found myself identifying with these women wearing skirts and head coverings and following the rules. Watching them recite prayers within the tunnels at the Western Wall and seeing their tears, I was filled with questions. I wanted to know how they felt about the God they worshipped.

My connection started in the Philadelphia airport as we were waiting to board our plane to Tel Aviv. Prepared for our thirteen-hour flight through the night, I was wearing a comfy knit skirt and leggings. I hadn't gotten my pixie cut yet, and my hair was past my shoulders. A teenage girl traveling with her father—who appeared to be an observant Jew—and also wearing a skirt, caught my eye across the room and smiled at me. It was a knowing smile, a smile I remembered, a smile reserved for someone you find out in the real world who is like you. I smiled back and felt my heart break.

We spent a couple of days in Jerusalem toward the end of our trip, and I was able to ask some of my questions. What I discovered surprised me. There were similarities between my experiences and those of the religious Jews I talked with, but our understanding of God was completely different. Even though they believed in following the law, and even though they didn't believe that Jesus was the Messiah, these people saw Jehovah primarily as a God of love and mercy. They had a fear of God, but they weren't afraid.

How does that work? How can we fear and yet not fear? It seems like modern Christianity often gets stuck in one of two extremes. Either zealous Christians get obsessed with Old Testament theology, or progressive Christians want to dismiss the Old Testament God as irrelevant and just talk about a loving Jesus. As people, we are so quick to stuff God into our little god-boxes. We want to explain Him, minimize Him, dismiss Him, and move on. We act like we have God all figured out. But what if we are wrong? What if we are terrifyingly wrong?

I'll say it again: the real God is not like us, my friends. We were simply made a little bit like Him. Listen to this beautiful passage from the prophet Isaiah (Isaiah 40:18, 21–26 NIV).

> With whom, then, will you compare God? To what image will you liken him? . . . Do you not know? Have you not heard? Has it not been told you from the beginning? Have you not understood since the earth was founded? He sits enthroned above the circle of the earth, and its people are like grasshoppers. He stretches out the heavens like a canopy, and spreads them out like a tent to live in. He brings princes to naught and reduces the rulers of this world to nothing. No sooner are they planted, no sooner are they sown, no sooner do they take root in the ground, than he blows on them and they wither, and a whirlwind sweeps them away like chaff. "To whom will you compare me? Or who is my equal?" says the Holy One. Lift up your eyes and look to the heavens: Who created all these? He who brings out the starry host one by one and calls forth each of them by name. Because of his great power and mighty strength, not one of them is missing.

A few years ago, back when my husband was a youth pastor, we watched a video with the youth group by Frances Chan. In the video, Francis Chan was concerned with the way the church has downplayed the idea of fear into mere reverence, respect, or awe. And it's true. The church as a whole doesn't talk much about a God who is frighteningly more than we can ever imagine. Too often we treat God like we would the CEO of a company or the president of a country. They have a more powerful position than we do, and so we give them a little more respect. God has our respect in our minds, but we aren't scared of Him. What does a healthy fear of God look like? Can we feel scared simply because of Who He is without being afraid of what He will do to us?

The Bible gives us plenty of examples of people having visions of God and falling on their faces in total fear. I'm pretty sure we would feel the same way if we ever saw Him face to face. And yet this same God continually walked and talked with people and ultimately revealed Himself to us as a humble servant in the Person of Jesus Christ. The real God is both/and, which makes Him even bigger, and wilder, and more fear-inspiring than ever.

Maybe I'm crazy, but I like this kind of God. I long for this kind of God. I want Him to be bigger, and holier, and more powerful, and *more* than I can ever imagine. I want to be terrified. I want to fall on my face before Him. I want to know that I am nothing and He is everything. I want this healthy fear to help guide the way I live, read His Word, and pursue Him. I want it to motivate the way I share His truth with others.

If God is actually real, a Person and not just a concept, and if He is really more powerful and awesome than I can imagine, then that truth changes everything. It changes my view of reality, which changes how I live. Not because I'm afraid of what God will do to me, but because of Who He is.

Because this very real God isn't only huge and scary; He is also incredibly good, and unconditionally loving, and incomprehensibly gracious, and more than we can ever imagine. And He wants me. He wants you. He wants a relationship with us. As often as the Bible talks about fearing God, it also says "don't be afraid." It's like we get to this point where we realize who He is, and we are rightfully terrified, but then God smiles and opens His arms. He is that big and overwhelming, but we don't have to be afraid. Because God is for us. He is on our side.

So, what do we do? How do we live in this place of tension and paradox? How do we fear God and yet not be afraid? I think we start by letting God out of our god-box. He doesn't fit in there anyway. We read the whole Bible and stop thinking we are smart enough to decide which parts are true or not. We realize that we are the creation and He is the Creator. We ask God to show us who He really is—so that we will fear Him. And we bask in the wonder that we can call this amazing Being our Daddy and our Friend.

WE CAN FEAR GOD FOR WHO HE IS
WITHOUT BEING AFRAID OF WHAT HE WILL DO.

PART THREE
REBUILDING OUR FAITH

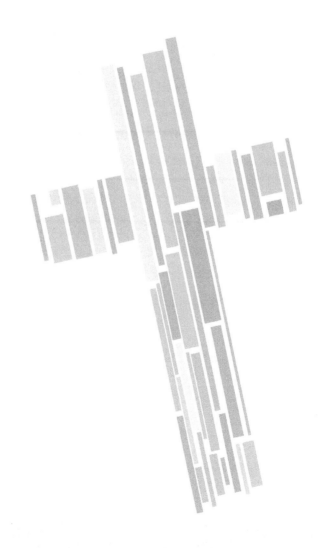

11

RECONCILING GOD AND JESUS

He slumped on the couch across from us, almost as though trying to absorb into its cushions as he admitted the truth. "I love
Jesus, but I am not okay with the God of the Old Testament." The
pain in his heart was written across his face along with confusion
and shame.

It was not the first time I'd heard this kind of thing expressed.
And I got it, because I'd been there too. Jesus is hard to hate,
unless of course you are a religious leader bent on earning your
way to God. Even other religions recognize Jesus Christ as being
a good man, a kind teacher, and an example to follow. But Jehovah, the God of the Old Testament? He seems to do some pretty
terrible things, things that are difficult to understand in our
twenty-first-century culture. He often appears distant, harsh, and
demanding. How in the world do we reconcile the angry, aloof
Jehovah of the Old Testament with the loving, gracious Jesus in
the New?

I've been taking some classes at my church on Sunday
nights—first on Bible Study Methods and now on the Torah. My

classes have been taught by a brilliant Hebrew scholar who is also
a professor at Dallas Theological Seminary. Learning from him
has forever changed how I will view the Old Testament.

We cannot read our English translation of this ancient piece
of literature in the modern world and assume that we understand
it correctly without help. There are so many differences that we
need to try to rectify before we can get a clear picture. Eastern
and Western culture, ancient and modern culture, original Hebrew idioms and other language challenges—these things and
more pose a huge challenge. Fortunately for us, we live in a world
where study tools are literally at our fingertips. Language and
culture differences explain most of the confusing parts if we take
the time to search and learn.

Spiritual abuse is often perpetrated by a misuse of the Old
Testament and a misrepresentation of the god that misuse reveals. Many of us have been deeply wounded by the picture of
god painted by people who were trying to control us through
fear. I understand why we would want to reject the Old Testament based on that abuse and our difficulty in understanding the
ancient culture and pictures of God it presents. But rather than
reject it, I'd love to see us try to reframe and embrace this history
of God and humanity. What if we were able to rediscover the God
of the Old Testament through Jesus?

Jesus isn't only a representation of God, He is God in human
form. And while a bigger picture of God is revealed as the Scriptures progress, God Himself doesn't change. "He [the Son] is the
image of the invisible God, the firstborn of all creation" (Colossians 1:15).

It's easy to think that Jesus shows up in Scripture when He
was born of the virgin in Matthew chapter one. But the Bible
is pretty clear that Jesus was intimately involved in speaking
the world into existence, and most Bible scholars agree that He
shows up periodically throughout the Old Testament as a theoph-
any (God coming in human form). While we can't imperatively
prove that any of these revelations are Jesus, they are in the least

a foreshadowing of the incarnation that will happen. Let's walk through a couple of these examples and talk about what they reveal to us about God.

ıı⁵ẫ⁸ı∎

We were made to be magnificent. Human beings were the culmination of God's creation. He lovingly, personally fashioned us from dust, intentionally sculpted and gave us life. Beautiful, powerful, creative, intelligent, and capable, we were built in the very image of God. We were especially designed for relationships—able to intimately know others and able to walk with God Himself—until it all fell apart.

I told you that we were going to talk about stories of Jesus in the Old Testament. Are you wondering what we are doing back in the garden of Eden again? Well, this is where Jesus starts. This is where the Gospel begins.

"In the beginning was the Word, and the Word was with God, and the Word was God. He was in the beginning with God. All things were made through him, and without him was not any thing made that was made. In him was life, and the life was the light of men" (John 1:1–4).

Surprisingly, Eden is where we first discover the nature of God and the nature of ourselves. It's where we first experience grace. I'd go so far as to say that without the garden of Eden, there is no Gospel of Jesus Christ.

"Now the serpent was more crafty than any other beast of the field that the LORD God had made. He said to the woman, 'Did God actually say, "You shall not eat of any tree in the garden"? . . . You will not surely die. For God knows that when you eat of it your eyes will be opened, and you will be like God, knowing good and evil'" (Genesis 3:1, 4–5).

The problem wasn't just that Adam and Eve disobeyed and ate the fruit. As we've said before, it's never simply about our outward actions. No, they doubted God's character. They wondered if He was really good, and if He was holding out on them. They believed the Enemy's lie and chose to do it their own way.

The knowledge of good and evil consumed Adam and Eve. They realized they were naked, tried to fix the problem with fig leaves, and ultimately hid from their Creator and Friend. Does this sound familiar? We humans have been living like this ever since. We still believe lies about God. We still doubt His character. We still choose to go our own way. We continue to try and fix our brokenness by ourselves. And we often hide ourselves from the presence of God.

I hear people talk about how at our core we are wretched sinners, that brokenness is our real identity. I also hear other people violently react to that teaching, choosing to see people as essentially good. I believe that at our core lies beauty and magnificence, but it's been mangled and perverted because of the sin that is also now a part of us. We all hold brokenness that we cannot escape. This is the nature of our humanity. We glimpse the potential, and we come face to face with the perversion every day. We cannot fix ourselves, and without God there is no hope. But when people ruined everything, God stepped in.

If He was really the God of anger and punishment that some people make Him out to be, Jehovah would have killed Adam and Eve and started over. He had every right to do so. They broke the rule and destroyed His perfect creation. He had promised death if they chose to disobey. Instead, God sought them. He called to them. He drew them out of hiding and to Himself.

"But the LORD God called to the man and said to him, 'Where are you?'" (Genesis 3:9).

God reached out to His broken, magnificent creations with questions He already knew the answer to. In gentleness and love He gave consequences for their disobedience. There had to be consequences. But amid the curses, there was also a promise. A human who would someday destroy the power of the serpent. And instead of guaranteed death falling on Adam and Eve, it fell

on the animals God used to make clothing for them. A picture
of a Savior who would one day substitute His life for ours.

So here is the question, Who is this God in the Garden? A
God who has feet to walk with the people He created and footsteps that they can hear? A God who seeks the broken? Does
He sound familiar to you? I think it's been Jesus from the very
beginning.

"For the Son of Man came to seek and to save the lost"
(Luke 19:10).

Slowly the old man trudged up the trail, his feet weighed down
more by dread than age. One hand clutched his staff, the other
stroked a piece of flint he carried in his pocket. He could feel
the knife on his belt bump against him with every step. Behind
him strode a boy just stepping into manhood. Lean and agile,
he hardly seemed to notice the weight of the wood strapped
to his back. With eager eyes and sure feet, the hike up Mount
Moriah was more adventure than effort for him. Suddenly, the
boy stopped.

"Father, I am carrying the wood for the sacrifice, and you
have the knife and flint. But, where is the lamb?"

The old man sighed, and a tear trickled down his leathery
face. Little did his boy know what was about to happen. His heart
threatened to break within him, yet, the father held on to hope.
It had been a long and sometimes difficult journey becoming a
friend of the Most High God. There had been many failures along
the way, but Abraham had learned one thing. El Elyon could be
trusted; His promises were true. And so, the old man drew a deep
breath and spoke from a heart of faith.

"God will provide the lamb for the offering, my son."

And He did! Right as Abraham was about to sacrifice his
beloved only son, God stepped in and provided a substitution.

"So Abraham called the name of that place, 'The LORD will provide'; as it is said to this day, 'On the mount of the LORD it shall be provided'" (Genesis 22:14).

I have heard this beautiful story used over and over again in moralistic or formulaic ways, and maybe you have too. "What are you holding back from God?" they ask. "What is your Isaac that God wants you to sacrifice?" Then they promise, "When you give things to God, He will give them back."

While I agree that we can learn things from the life of Abraham and that we can indeed apply this account to our own lives, I also believe that moralistic religion misses the main point of the story. The New Testament tells us in James 2:23 that Abraham believed God and that his belief was counted as righteousness. He was called a friend of God.

Abraham believed God, except the funny thing is that he didn't. At least not all the time. Abraham is listed in the hall of faith in Hebrews eleven, but if you read his story in Genesis twelve to twenty-two, you will see more instances of doubt than of faith. Twice Abraham pretended that his wife was his sister and allowed her to be taken into a harem. He fathered a child with his servant because he doubted God's promise and then abandoned them both in the desert. Abraham wasn't some super spiritual giant of the faith. He was simply a guy who became friends with God. What if that's the point?

Years before the Law, before the sacrifices, before the temple, before Jesus died on the cross, there was a man who became friends with God. It wasn't because of the rules he followed, or disciplines he undertook, or any of his outward actions. Abraham had a relationship with God through faith.

He talked with God, followed God, questioned God, doubted God, and saw God do miracles. Eventually, after a lifetime of this relationship, Abraham was at a place where he knew the Most High so well, and his faith was so strong, that he was willing to do the unthinkable and sacrifice his only son. But it didn't happen, because the angel of the Lord stepped in.

"But the angel of the LORD called to him from heaven . . . 'Do not lay your hand on the boy'" (Genesis 22:11–12).

The angel of the Lord is the one who showed up all throughout Abraham's life. He was the one Abraham met, fed, talked to, argued with, and the one who ultimately stopped his sacrifice. So, who is this angel of the Lord? Are you ready for this? Most theologians believe that the angel of the Lord is pre-incarnate Jesus. Jesus. But it gets better.

Roughly two thousand years later, Mount Moriah—the mountain where Abraham almost sacrificed Isaac—had been developed into a city named Jerusalem. One spring, on the outskirts of that city, a controversial rabbi was crucified. "On the mount of the LORD it shall be provided," Abraham declared. And it was.

"For God so loved the world, that he gave his only Son, that whoever believes in him should not perish but have eternal life. For God did not send his Son into the world to condemn the world, but in order that the world might be saved through him. Whoever believes in him is not condemned, but whoever does not believe is condemned already, because he has not believed in the name of the only Son of God" (John 3:16–18).

Jesus has always been Jesus. The God whose name is I AM does not change. The Jesus that we shake our heads at—yet adore—in the New Testament, is the same in the Old. If you look closely, you will recognize Him: the God who pursues, forgives, loves, gives grace, and sacrifices Himself for the sins of the world. He is powerful, amazing, crazy, confusing, addicting, and beautiful. Will you seek Him with me? I've got one more story to share.

▌▐▐▌▐▌▌

The nation of Israel was in exile in Babylon. It shouldn't have been a surprise. When God made His original covenant with this people group, He warned them what would happen if they disobeyed. Patiently, God waited and gave grace for hundreds of years while they occasionally sought Him but mostly did their own thing. Now the nation had been conquered by the mighty King Nebuchadnezzar of Babylon.

The book of Daniel opens with some painful details. Jerusalem had been captured, the temple was in ruins, and young noblemen had been collected to serve as eunuchs in the palace of Nebuchadnezzar. If Jehovah of the Old Testament was as harsh or judgmental as some people claim He is, then we would not see the story that unfolds.

Despite the fact that the temple was in ruins and the sacrifices were no longer being made, God still pursued a relationship with individual people. Even though the nation as a whole had rejected God and His commands, somehow three young men knew the truth about Jehovah and had a relationship with Him. Here in this place of oppression, suffering, and exile, we still find a loving God pursuing the people He has created without requiring behaviors or sacrifices. Instead, it came down to their faith.

Caught tight within the shifting crowd, Shadrach, Meshach, and Abednego were three dots in a sea of people gathered in this open plain. They were all there for one purpose: to worship a large and elaborate statue of the king. Around ninety feet tall, the golden image glittered with impressive but deadly beauty. Musicians had assembled at the base of the statue and were preparing to play. Shadrach caught Meshach and Abednego's eyes; "Here we go," his look said. With a burst of sound, the music began and the crowds surrounding these three men fell to the ground, faces in the dirt, paying homage to the glittering statue. Three bodies stayed awkwardly and noticeably upright.

Do you know how to make a prideful, power-hungry narcissist angry? Refuse to do what he says in front of other people. It will work every time. King Nebuchadnezzar was furious. How dare these conquered Israelites defy his commands? Demanding that Shadrach, Meshach, and Abednego be brought to face him, Nebuchadnezzar feigned mercy and gave them one more chance to worship him. Refusal would mean death. This is a familiar story and you probably know how it ends.

The three Hebrew men declared to this powerful, conquering king that Jehovah, God of Israel, could save them from the fiery furnace. But even if He didn't, they still wouldn't worship Nebuchadnezzar's golden statue. In an insane rage, the Babylonian king fired up his furnaces seven times hotter than normal, so hot that the flames killed the soldiers who threw Shadrach, Meshach, and Abednego inside the fires. Then Nebuchadnezzar waited to see what would happen. And suddenly he rubbed his eyes in disbelief. There were no longer only three men walking around in the furnace, there were four, and the fourth one looked different—like a son of the gods.

Did Jesus walk in the fire with Shadrach, Meshach, and Abednego? Very possibly, although it's impossible to prove. But more importantly, we see a relationship with God based on faith. It's always been about faith and it's never been about works. Shadrach, Meshach, and Abednego were not saved from the fire because of their good, religious behavior. It wasn't because they refused to bow to an idol. God chose to save them because He wanted to, because He wanted to display His divine power to Nebuchadnezzar (who years later would have his own encounter with the Living God). The three Hebrew men had faith in the very real God they knew even though they could've died in the furnace. This story is not about outcomes or performance, it's about a relationship. It's always been about a relationship.

We need the Old Testament along with the New Testament to get a clear picture of the history of God and the people He created. We need to see God's holiness, power, and authority so that we will fully appreciate Jesus's love and grace. It's okay that some of the Old Testament doesn't make sense to us automatically. It's an ancient book written from a completely different cultural background. But my hope is that as you read it for yourself, in context, and with study tools, you will discover that Jesus is revealed within its pages.

JESUS IS HIDING IN THE OLD TESTAMENT IF WE LOOK FOR HIM.

12

BELIEVING IN RADICAL LOVE

The first time I saw Freddie, he was literally being dragged into the principal's office by his ear. I didn't even know that really happened anymore, but apparently it does when you are a desperate gym teacher who is sick and tired of dealing with Freddie. I was shelving books in the middle school library and heard the commotion through the big glass windows that looked out into the hall. Freddie had his own reputation, but it didn't hurt that he was also the youngest Ellis boy. Everyone in our small town knew about the Ellis clan. They were infamous.

Freddie and I were about as different as you could get. Although I'd moved past my terror of the public school system, I still wore long jean jumpers and waist-length hair as I volunteered twice a week at our local middle school. I was a home-schooled-in-a-cult, sheltered twenty-year-old. Freddie was a messed-up eighth-grader from a family of known felons and drug addicts. But I loved him.

There was no reason for me to love Freddie; he was not loveable. The teachers sighed when they said his name, and everyone was relieved on the days he skipped school. I wasn't even volunteering with eighth-grade students because they were much too scary in my opinion. I mostly read with struggling fifth-graders and shelved books for the librarian. But my heart broke for Freddie, the naughtiest, scariest eighth-grader of all.

His resource room teacher thought I was crazy when I asked if she needed help with him, but she handed me some work he hadn't finished and let me take Freddie back to the library. Freddie thought I was crazy too, but he was happy to get out of class. And that's how we started working together. On the afternoons I came to school, I'd walk down to see if Freddie was there and we'd head back to the library together for half an hour or so. Sometimes he worked. Sometimes he poked himself with pencils and scribbled on his papers until they had holes. And sometimes we talked.

"Why are you here if you don't get paid?" Freddie asked me one day.

"Because I love kids," I replied.

"Even druggies like me?"

"Especially kids like you."

Freddie doesn't have a happy ending to his story. I didn't save him, or turn him around, or help him to do something with his life. I left town at the end of that school year for college and I never saw him again. But Freddie changed me. Because God used Freddie to show me what unconditional love looks like. Jesus poured His love for Freddie into my heart and I couldn't help myself. And when I thought about how bad Freddie was and yet how much I loved him for no reason, I often heard a quiet whisper, "That's how I love you."

Growing up, I thought that God loved me more when I was performing well—when I was following the rules and towing the line. Then I met Freddie, and I realized that God loved me despite my mess. Maybe even because of it. God's love for us is ridiculous, scandalous, and for no reason except that He chooses to love because that's who He is.

"See what great love the Father has lavished on us, that we should be called children of God!" (1 John 3:1 NIV).

Something lavish is excessive, more than necessary, and over the top. Loving people who don't deserve it makes God's love even more powerful and crazy. But I'm pretty sure Jesus likes that about Himself. He has always been all about the broken and lost. Why is it so hard for us to see ourselves that way? To realize that we are Freddie?

My grandpa loved burned cookies. That last pan that got forgotten in the oven, the extra crispy ones with the hard brown edges that no one else wanted to eat—those were his favorites. When my grandparents came to visit, he always had the same question for my mom. "Got any burned cookies?"

At first I thought he was joking or trying to make my mom feel better if she'd burned any. But as I grew up, I realized that my grandpa was serious. With thirteen children in the family, Grandpa's mom was a little busy, and burned cookies were often the result. Strangely Grandpa not only got used to burned cookies, but he preferred them. I recently learned that various relatives would often burn a pan for him on purpose. That makes me laugh.

And it makes me think of Jesus. As people, especially in our virtual world of social media, we value having it together. It's important that we are looking good, behaving well, or at least faking it. But while He was on earth, Jesus seemed to prefer the broken ones, choosing to make rejected people His closest friends. He was always pursuing the outcasts and the obvious sinners. I think He was a little bit like my grandpa. I love imagining Jesus coming in with outstretched hands and a smile, "I'm here for the broken ones."

We're all broken. Some of us are just better at hiding it than others. The tax collectors and prostitutes that Jesus befriended weren't any worse sinners than the Pharisees. Sin isn't only outward behaviors. The church today desperately needs a bigger understanding of sin as well as a deeper grasp of God's love. I think religious Christians often see sin as merely behaviors they need to avoid. Somehow the goal has become outward goodness, and our real issues get shoved under the rug and into the closet. Guilt and shame keep them there, and as a result, many church people never get to fully comprehend grace. God didn't save us to make us good people. He saved us because we were dead by ourselves and needed life. He saved us because we were lost and needed to be found.

Sin isn't simply bad behavior. It's the deep self-centeredness that discolors everything. It's in our thoughts, attitudes, and the motives of our hearts. We cannot get rid of it by ourselves, but we don't have to. God doesn't want good people. How's that for a crazy thought? God does not value human efforts at goodness. It is utterly impossible for us ever to be good enough on our own.

But this is why the Gospel is good news. Jesus loves broken people, messed-up ones, and total failures. And those are the kinds of people who love Him back. Because they know they need Him. Because they know they can't do it on their own. Because they come humbly to the cross and accept His free gift of forgiveness. When we are broken, we are able to be healed. When we are lost, we are able to be found. When we are total sinners, we are able to experience forgiveness. In humility we find lavish grace, mercy, and love.

∎│∎│∎│∎│∎

I recently reread a theological fantasy series called The Archives of Anthropos by the late Christian author, psychiatrist, and pastor John White. I first read it as a teenager, and then again to my husband shortly after we were married. But reading it now a decade later, I'm struck afresh by the wisdom and truth that John White weaves through his stories.

In the first book, there is a boy who is supposed to be the Bearer. He has an impressive sword and a mission to accomplish. But because he stubbornly refuses to drink the wine of free pardon, he cannot get his sword to leave the scabbard. He is powerless on his own, and yet in pride he refuses to accept the power of the Changer. I'm so irritated with his character and yet so convicted at the same time. I find it ironic that the only thing that stops God's loving grace is our stubborn pride.

No sinner is too sinful for God's grace. We can never be too far away from it. Yet He allows us to resist. He wants to give us the kingdom, but He won't push anything on us. We often think of pride as feeling superior—like we don't need God or His grace and that we are fine on our own. But reverse pride is just as dangerous, maybe even more so. Reverse pride is deciding that we are too messed up, too bad, or too far away for God to reach. That somehow, we are outside of God's loving grace.

The wine of free pardon is available to anyone in Anthropos. The initial sip is full of bitterness and fire, but those who choose to drink deeply are filled with inexplicable joy and peace. They receive supernatural healing and strength. This picture resonates with me.

Surrendering to God's grace, admitting we need it and that we have nothing to offer in return, is humbling. And letting go of control can be terrifying because control brings feelings of safety. But God's grace is amazing. It's beyond our wildest imagination. Free pardon is based totally on Jesus and on not at all on me. It's crazy, insane, and beautiful. And once you've tasted it, you can't go back. Not only grace for salvation, but grace for life. Grace is not just a word or a concept, it's a force.

I wish there was something I could do or say to convince everyone to jump into the ocean that is God's grace. To leave our pride, stubbornness, and control on the top of the cliff and jump: screaming, eyes shut, arms flung wide. To let God love us like He loves Freddie, like He loves burned cookies, like He loves His broken and beautiful world.

But God does not force us. He will woo us, draw us, and tantalize us, but ultimately, He allows us to decide. And if we choose to stubbornly resist, He lets us.

I think that there are many in the church who have experienced grace for salvation and called it good. We don't know what we are missing. Receiving the full force of God's grace doesn't take any action on our part except for repentance and an open hand.

Repentance means that we agree with God. We admit our pride, fear, and desire for control. We agree that those things are holding us back and that they are wrong. Then, with head bowed and (most likely) teary eyes, we open our hands and let God overwhelm us with His grace. This is not about us; it's about Him. Let me share one more story to convince you.

I probably should have been scared. He was very noticeable standing at the Starbucks counter. Not only was he was dressed all in black with tall black combat boots, but he also had this amazing hair. It might have been fake, but it was really long, black, almost like dreads, and kind of jagged. As I got closer, I saw the black gauges in his ears, and not one but two rings through the center of his nose. I smiled.

Standing behind him as he ordered, I was close enough to see his chains, tattoos, and black, zippered leather jacket. My smile got bigger. We waited for our coffee together, although he never looked up from his phone. From the front, I could see the satanic goat head on his black ball cap, and I caught a glimpse of the death metal T-shirt under his jacket. By this point, I was almost in tears. I could hardly contain the love I felt for this beautiful, broken human that I'd never even met. He didn't acknowledge me. But I do have to wonder if he noticed the overly-happy woman watching him with a stupid grin on her face.

I sat in my car for a minute, sipping my coffee, tears trickling down my face, praying for this stranger that I now loved. The Holy Spirit began to whisper again. "I see you just like that, Christy— every bit of hurt, brokenness, mess with such clarity—and I love you even more than you can imagine. I see you, and I think, 'How beautiful! What a beautiful, broken mess.'"

It's one thing to read the Bible and believe that God loves us. But this is how I am completely convinced of God's loving adoration. Sometimes He lets me feel a little bit of His heart. God's love is passionate and ridiculous, intense and crazy. We don't even have an English word to describe the power of the love He feels for us. There was no reason for me to love that tall, skinny, potentially satanic, black-clad young man that I'd never met before. But I did because the God of the universe loves him beyond words. And He loves you too. You are loved and liked by the Creator of the Cosmos.

We are all broken. That's the absolute truth. I think this is one of the reasons I love alternative types of people so much—they are brave enough to wear their brokenness openly. The rest of us scramble around, pretending we have it all together. We fake it, hoping to be believable. Trying to fool other people, ourselves, and God, we find more socially acceptable ways to be screwed up. But there is no shame in being broken, not in the arms of Jesus. No condemnation. He already knows our deepest, darkest secrets, and He doesn't care. They do nothing to affect His love for us. If anything, maybe our brokenness makes Him love us even more. Think about it, what takes more love? Loving someone who is good, wonderful, perfect, and easy to love? Or loving someone who couldn't care less about you, who is your enemy, who hurts you, and runs away?

Being broken is part of being human thanks to our sinful nature. What if we could accept it? What if we could truly believe that it's okay? And then what if we could bring those broken pieces to the foot of the cross and be healed. It's not by our own efforts because that would be like trying to reconstruct a broken piece of China with Scotch tape. We are healed by the blood of Jesus Christ. His grace, His forgiveness, His death and resurrection. When Jesus fixes us, it's like kintsugi.

Are you familiar with this word? Kintsugi is an ancient Japanese art of fixing broken ceramic pieces. They use a special lacquer dusted with powdered gold, silver, or platinum. When artists glue the pieces back together, seams of gold glitter in the cracks of the ceramic, giving a uniquely beautiful appearance to each piece. This method of repair celebrates each artifact's unique history by emphasizing its fractures instead of disguising or hiding them. Kintsugi often makes the repaired piece even more beautiful than the original and what was once shattered is given new life.

Jesus wants to gather our broken pieces into His arms and love us exactly the way we are. Then He wants to put us back together. We tend to think God is looking for perfection and we feel our inadequacy. But Jesus gives us His perfection when we trust in His work on the cross. God sees us as perfect because of Jesus's death. We are broken, and yet we are whole. In the same way that kintsugi emphasizes the gold lines fixing the cracked pottery, when people look at us, they will see Jesus.

"We have this treasure in jars of clay, to show that the surpassing power belongs to God and not to us" (2 Corinthians 4:7).

THE LOVE OF GOD IS RIDICULOUSLY LAVISH AND MAKES NO SENSE.

13

LEARNING TO YIELD

What the serpent said made sense—maybe Eve was confused. Maybe she had misunderstood God's original instructions; or maybe Adam hadn't shared them clearly with her. The fruit was beautiful to look at. The more she stared, the more enticing it became. If this tree would make them more like God, then why would God keep this knowledge from them? Surely, eating the fruit was the right thing to do. Yes friends, we are back in the garden of Eden for the third time.

The Tree of Knowledge of Good and Evil offered an elusive promise. Forgetting they were already made in God's image, and thinking they were becoming more like God, Adam and Eve listened to the serpent's words. Deceived, they believed they were making the good choice. Ironically, choosing to disobey God and eat from the tree immediately perverted the knowledge Adam and Eve gained. As humans, we now have the capacity to know good and evil, but can we really differentiate between the two? I'm honestly not sure we can.

Growing up in my ultra-conservative version of Christianity, many normal behaviors were considered evil. Listening to rock music, dating, going to college, women wearing pants, men growing beards, being friends with the opposite gender, women working outside the home—all of these things were bad. And that didn't even include going to movie theaters, drinking alcohol, getting tattoos, or having multiple piercings. If you don't come from a conservative background, this list of *evil things* might seem ridiculous. But look at extreme versions of any religion and you will find the same scenario. In a frenzied desire for holiness, normal and good things become bad.

The opposite is also true. People call plenty of hurtful, damaging, truly evil things good. I don't even need to make a list of the behaviors and attitudes we see in our world, because just reading that sentence brought them to your mind. We know that there is such a thing as good and evil, but our ability to distinguish the two has been perverted. Unfortunately, it gets worse.

In our brokenness, we not only want to classify behaviors as good or bad, but we also want to classify people. This is where we really screw things up. Differences can be scary and uncomfortable. If your beliefs or looks or actions are different from mine, then you must be wrong. You must be bad. It is true that everyone has been broken by sin, but different isn't the same as bad. Different isn't wrong. It's just different and that's okay. Then there's our motives.

Motives can make good behavior bad. Prayer, Bible reading, church attendance, Scripture memorization, giving, serving, all of these things are good, right? Not when they are done to gain something, or to prove something, or to pridefully show off amazing spirituality. When our motives are evil, then our good actions are no longer good.

But people can also do bad actions with good motives. If the bad things they do are motivated by a desire for justice, or because of intense hurt, are they really bad? Does it make them bad people?

This knowledge of good and evil is harder than it sounds, isn't it? Our world is broken and the people in it have been corrupted by sin. It's a mess. A dark, confusing, depressing mess. But into that darkness came the Light.

"The true light, which gives light to everyone, was coming into the world. He was in the world, and the world was made through him, yet the world did not know him. He came to his own, and his own people did not receive him. But to all who did receive him, who believed in his name, he gave the right to become children of God" (John 1:9–12).

Jesus lived as the only perfect person to walk our little planet. He defied human laws, norms, and expectations. He loved people no one else would look at. Everything he did was right and good, even though sometimes it looked wrong. He was God in a human body, but the religious leaders said he was possessed by the devil. They missed the Messiah because he didn't fit their ideas of good and evil. These religious leaders murdered an innocent man, convincing the Romans to crucify him even though they couldn't find fault. And yet, that horrific act of evil was the best thing that ever happened. Because, as Jesus drew his last breath, as his blood dripped down, He provided forgiveness for the world. He became our Savior.

The world is broken. We are broken. The sooner we realize that, the better off we will be. We desperately need Jesus. He is the only hope. The good news is, we can have Him. He offers Himself as a free gift for the taking.

Since we are terrible at truly discerning good from evil, and our fixation on correct behaviors only brings death, maybe we should focus instead on love. How can I love God with everything I am? And then how can I truly love my neighbor? What if we will find true good and evil as we genuinely seek to love God and others by the power of the Holy Spirit?

Understanding that we struggle to know good and evil is the first step in having a clear understanding of how to live as a follower of Jesus. If it's not about behavior and performance, and if God's grace is a free gift, then how do we walk out this relationship we have with God?

I got into a heated online discussion a while back over an article called "9 Sins the Church Is Surprisingly Okay With as Long as You Love Jesus." A Christian influencer posted a link to the article and asked what their followers thought. Although initially skeptical, I perused the article anyway. I didn't get further than their supposed nine sins (fear, apathy, gluttony, worry, flattery, comfort, consumerism, patriotism, and lying) before I started feeling frustrated. Sure, some of those things could be considered sins and all of them can be bad for you, but really? I could feel an overwhelming pile of guilt and shame on my head and I hadn't even finished the article. I posted a comment expressing my feelings.

I'm not sure I agree with all the points in this article. I don't think that all of them are truly sins. But I do agree that all of these can be cured by a genuine relationship with Jesus. Not religion, not rules, not trying harder, not human effort, but meeting the Person of Jesus Christ. Getting to know Him, falling in love with Him, and choosing to follow Him, because Jesus changes everything.

Surprisingly, that comment became the most popular. And then the disagreement started because people were quickly offended by my supposed acceptance of sin. "You are deceived when you don't know the scriptures," they told me. "You need to know Jesus, the Character of God, and your views will change. Otherwise, you will suckle milk and look like you do for a very, very, very long time." Nice. Thanks. Did you even read my comment?

The personal disagreement didn't bother me. I like a good, healthy discussion. But what did bother me was the harsh comments on the post. People were pretty mean. And those struggling with anxiety disorders and depression left the conversation feeling judged and condemned. Lots of the comments sure didn't sound like Jesus, yet they came from people who claimed His name.

I had to step away and take some time to process. And I found myself asking a question. Why do we choose to do right and to stop sinning? Is it because we are afraid of making God angry or disappointed? Are we trying to keep God happy? Is it so that we will look good to other people? Are we trying to maintain a good testimony so that people will think we are godly?

I find there are often two sides within Christianity: the rule-followers and the no-rulers. The rule-followers call the no-rulers worldly and licentious (which is a big word that means they don't follow the rules). The no-rulers call the rule-followers closed-minded and legalistic. What if they are both wrong? How do we find a middle ground of grace and truth?

Paul told the Galatians that it is for freedom Christ has set us free and we are to stand firm in it. We should not let ourselves be burdened again by a yoke of slavery. Jesus wants us to be free. He died to set us free. Free from rules, and free from sin. We don't have to live as slaves to rules, trying to appease God and avoid His judgment. Jesus already took God's wrath and the judgment for sin on Himself. Once we trust that Jesus took the punishment for our sin, we have access to a relationship with a God who loves us unconditionally.

But neither do we have to live as slaves of sin. We don't have to be controlled by our habits, addictions, and natural tendencies any longer. When Jesus died, He set us free from the punishment of sin, but also from the power of sin. He has given us His Holy Spirit to live inside of us and empower us to follow Him.

■ | ■ ▪ ■ | ■

With a traitorous profession and a sketchy reputation, Zacchaeus definitely wasn't a model Jewish citizen. Everyone knew that he had become wealthy by working as a tax collector for the Romans and cheating his fellow Jews out of their money. Zacchaeus was a Jew by blood, but the religious Pharisees considered him a condemned sinner since he didn't follow the Law or

Jewish traditions. But on this day, a strange rabbi who also had a reputation was passing through the area and Zacchaeus was curious. In Luke nineteen we read that he was seeking to see who Jesus was.

Unfortunately Zacchaeus had a height problem. Unable to even catch a glimpse of Jesus within the crowds, he climbed a nearby tree. Perched at the edge of the road, isolated from the crush and noise, Zacchaeus was ready for Jesus to pass by. But Jesus was also seeking. He was seeking for a messed-up, too short, social traitor and religious outcast. Jesus deliberately stopped by the tree, looked up at Zacchaeus—smiled, I'm sure—and said, "Zacchaeus, hurry up and come down, for today I must stay at your place."

Had Jesus lost His mind? The crowd's grumbling reaction tells us how crazy this was. Jesus boldly announced that He was going to intentionally hang out with an obvious sinner. But Jesus didn't give Zacchaeus a list of rules to follow. He didn't condemn him, or reject him, or tell him to clean up his act. Jesus sought, accepted, loved, and demonstrated His desire to build a relationship with Zacchaeus. And something interesting happened. Face-to-face with the real God, Zacchaeus fell apart.

"Watch me, Lord! Right now, I give half of my possessions to the poor, and if I have cheated anybody out of anything, I will pay them back four times the amount."

Jesus was delighted. Not because of the changed behaviors, not because of the list of right things Zacchaeus was going to do, but because salvation had been accomplished and Zacchaeus had been redeemed.

"Today," Jesus said, "Salvation has come to this household. For the Son of Man came to seek and save the lost."

The Son of Man came to seek and save the lost. That is amazing news. We are desperately lost, desperately broken, but it is okay because we are also desperately loved. We are insanely and scandalously adored. Jesus came specifically to seek and save us. He wants all of us, every bit of our broken pieces. He wants to forgive our sin and gently put us back together.

Coming face-to-face with the real Jesus will change us. But contrary to religious beliefs, change isn't the goal. The goal is knowing Jesus. Experiencing Him, believing Him, and allowing Him to make us into the very best version of ourselves. Religion, even Christian religion, is always about behavior, always about control. And religion never gets God right because it doesn't understand who He really is. The real Jesus doesn't control. He doesn't motivate us with guilt and shame. He draws us with loving-kindness. He patiently woos us. He seeks and saves the lost.

Here is some hard truth. If our version of Christianity is about anything or anyone other than Jesus, then it's probably wrong. If we think we are making God happy with our rule following, we aren't. If we care more about ourselves and our comfortable, satisfying life than we care about Jesus and developing a relationship with Him, we are missing the point. When our "Christianity" stops being about Jesus, His amazing grace, and our ability to know God through Jesus, it ceases to be true Christianity.

Which brings us back to the same question. Why do we choose to do what is right? If we aren't trying to appease God or earn anything, and if we aren't trying to impress others or make them happy with us, then what is our motivation?

I'll tell you my personal reasoning. It's because I love Jesus, but it's also because I don't like the consequences that come when I choose sin. Sin always has consequences, sometimes they are direct and sometimes they are more subtle, but they are always there. Sin brings death—which is separation from God, others, and ourselves—but Jesus gives life.

I remember going to Walmart in my long skirts and long hair and feeling holy compared to the rest of the world. I stood out. I was separate. I believed that people could tell I was truly following Jesus. I thought my walk would make them want God. But in reality they probably just thought I was weird. Holiness does mean set apart, but it doesn't mean doing outward stuff to make yourself stand out. It means that we have been set apart by God because He is transforming our hearts. These days I believe that true holiness looks more like surrender and less like works.

I first heard the words *surrender to the lordship of Jesus* on a podcast. The host and her guest were talking about laying aside really difficult things because of their love for Jesus. It felt different for some reason than the times I'd heard people talking about making Jesus Lord of their lives. The words were so similar, but the heart behind the words was so different. There was no condemnation or pressure in their voices. Instead I heard humility, a little sadness, but mostly love.

Making Jesus Lord intrinsically involves effort on my part. I am working to make Jesus Lord. There are things I am doing so that He will be Lord in my life. But surrendering to Jesus's lordship is a humble acknowledgment that He is already Lord. It is letting go of control and surrendering my desires while accepting His will for my life. *Making* is a forceful action verb. *Surrender* is passive. I really believe that surrender is the key to true holiness and obedience. And love makes surrender possible. When we understand how much God loves us, and how crazy amazing He is, we cannot help but love Him in return.

We cannot perform our way into freedom. Only Jesus can set us free, and it's only by the power of His death and resurrection. It's a part of our relationship with Him. As the Spirit of Jesus convicts our hearts of sin, we choose to repent and agree with Him. Then we choose to accept what He has already done, come alongside Him, and lay down our lives as well. It is only through surrender that the power of the Holy Spirit can be released in our lives.

"I pray that out of his glorious riches he may strengthen you with power through his Spirit in your inner being, so that Christ may dwell in your hearts through faith. And I pray that you, being rooted and established in love, may have power, together with all the Lord's holy people, to grasp how wide and long and high and deep is the love of Christ, and to know this love that surpasses knowledge—that you may be filled to the measure of all the fullness of God" (Ephesians 3:16–19).

OBEDIENCE IS ABOUT HUMILITY AND SURRENDER
RATHER THAN PERFORMANCE AND DUTY.

14

FINDING THE MISSING PIECE

"Is there anything wrong with that?" His voice was a gentle rumble that spoke to my soul. No, the answer could only be no, there was nothing wrong.

The knotty pine beams of the camp chapel arched overhead while the snow drifted down outside, and we sat mesmerized by this big black man leading us in an experience of God like we'd never had before. Johnny Jones had been a pastor before coming to serve at our cultic organization's newest training center in the city of Flint, Michigan. Unbeknownst to me at the time, he had been betrayed by the organization and was a broken man who would soon be leaving the center completely disillusioned. But before he went, Pastor Johnny came to teach at our winter youth retreat.

I wonder if it was Pastor Johnny's own frustration that fueled his passion that night. His own desperation for God that provided an avenue into the Spirit's power and presence. I wonder if his eyes had been opened to the lies and if he was trying to set us free too. Whatever it was, we felt it. And from his stool on the stage, Pastor Johnny led us in an experience that I will never forget.

God was there in that chapel with us. Someone would read a portion of Scripture, or pray, or start to sing, or whatever they felt prompted to do. And Johnny's deep rumble would gently ask us each time it was finished, "Is there anything wrong with that?"

"No," we whispered back.

I don't know what revival really looks like, but when I hear the word, I can't help thinking back to this snowy retreat in northern Michigan. Despite still being deep in the cult, I felt something that night that reinforced my own beliefs in the total reality of God. He was more than a distant concept or idea; He was a real and living presence.

My cultic church and the institute ignored the Holy Spirit, but I accidently discovered Him when I was seventeen. I loved to read dusty old books written by believers in the 1800s, and in one of them I found this phrase, "the secret of the miracle of the Christian life." I've spent years trying to figure out which author gave me that phrase, but I've come up short. Not even Google has been able to help.

What was this secret of the miracle of the Christian life? It was the Spirit of Jesus Christ from Romans chapter eight. The apostle Paul talks at length about living in the Spirit rather than living in the flesh, and this currently unknown, historical Christian author explained that life in the Spirit was possible as we chose to surrender to the Spirit and stop trying to do life by ourselves. In my world of strict rules and behaviors, this idea was a refreshing breath of oxygen. And so, I began to pray.

"Jesus, I cannot do this alone. I need You. Possess me. I want to live by your Spirit and not my own strength." And crazy things happened.

I found it much easier to be kind to my siblings and get along with my parents. I stopped having to think about rules so much because doing the right thing came more naturally. My heart was filled with joy and life. People noticed and asked questions. I told them it was Jesus. You can literally see a difference in my pictures from this time period. Yes, I was still in a Christian cult bound by standards of behavior, lies, and twisted Bible verses, but I was also alive on the inside. The Holy Spirit was moving and changing me with a power greater than myself.

It took years for me to connect the dots. Not long ago I was driving in my car alone pondering the Holy Spirit when I had an epiphany. My thoughts wandered down this path:

What happened to the Holy Spirit in evangelical Christianity? He definitely gets less than his fair share of attention. Theologically, the Holy Spirit is an equal member of the Trinity, but unless you attend a charismatic or Pentecostal church, He is pretty much ignored. Sure, we tell people that they will receive the Holy Spirit when they trust in Jesus to be their Savior. We might mention that He is called the Comforter or Helper (John 14:15–26) or that He is the guarantee of our salvation (2 Corinthians 1:21–22). But most of us don't talk about Him, and we definitely don't pray to Him.

Is it because we don't know what to do with the Holy Spirit? Maybe we're afraid of Him or unsure about Him, so we ignore Him. We talk about God and Jesus and leave it at that.

I sat there thinking, wishing I knew more about the Holy Spirit and feeling like I was missing something, when it hit me. According to the Bible, the Holy Spirit is the One I know the best. This realization was almost overwhelming.

The Bible tells us that God the Father is in Heaven. Jesus is in Heaven sitting at God's right hand. But the Holy Spirit, the Holy Spirit is the One here with us.

It's hard to explain the emotion that exploded in my heart. It was as if I'd grown up knowing I had a missing sibling and then suddenly found out that they had been my best friend for the past ten years. It was an "Oh, it's You!" moment.

I called Him *Jesus*, but it was actually the Holy Spirit who became real to me when I was fifteen years old, helped me to see through the lies within my cultic organization, and started my questioning and rebelling against the false teachings of my church. The Holy Spirit was the one who brought me to my Christian summer camp and helped me to find true grace, freedom, and love. He was the One I'd gotten to know over the years. I'd felt His Presence. We'd talked and laughed together. He explained the Bible to me and reminded me of verses I needed to hear. He was the One who gave me strength and peace through my miscarriages and helped me to trust when I didn't think I could. He helped me to deconstruct and reconstruct my Christian beliefs multiple times. He showed me how to forgive, let go, and move on. I called Him Jesus, but He was really the missing member of the Trinity, the Holy Spirit. I wasn't sure why this new understanding made me want to giggle, but it did. I was filled with an unexplainable joy and satisfaction.

What if the Holy Spirit is the solution to our problem of misunderstanding God? What if He is the solution to far more than that? Could acknowledging the Holy Spirit and working to build a relationship with Him stop us from getting sucked into behavior-driven religion? Would recognizing the Spirit's reality and presence open our eyes to the power of God? Could the Holy Spirit sort out our misunderstandings of Jesus and the Father? I'm eager to find out.

When I look at modern American churches, I often see one of two extremes in the way they deal with the Holy Spirit. He is either ignored like what I experienced growing up, or there is an attempt to control Him and harness His power for human gain. Rarely is the Holy Spirit acknowledged as God and given the respect, reverence, and even fear He is due. I wonder what would happen to the church if that changed. I wonder what would happen to us if that changed.

Maybe the Holy Spirit is uncomfortable to more conservative and fundamental churches because the Spirit isn't easily understandable or controllable. We can put God in a box, Jesus sort of goes in a box, but how in the world do you box the Spirit? He is untamed, wild, and free. And I suppose if you are trying to control your members through fear—either in a church or Christian cult—then making them aware of the very Spirit of God living inside of them and giving them power, wisdom, and knowledge might be a bad thing. It's very likely that you would lose your followers because they would begin to see through you and your lies. And if people recognize that they have a supernatural power living within them working to restore their very hearts, well, rules and standards are no longer as important. Human leaders begin to lose power when the Holy Spirit gets control.

Humans love power, let's be honest. So it makes sense to me that some people and churches would work to be able to harness and control the power of the Holy Spirit. But can the Holy Spirit truly be controlled? And is the power they claim to have really His? These are important questions to ask. One of my favorite Christian authors, Dr. John White, began to gravitate to more charismatic views later in life. But he was very aware of the difference between being conduits of God's power and trying to control it ourselves. In fact, in his spiritual fantasy series The Archives of Anthropos that I referenced earlier, every book makes a clear distinction between sorcerers who seek power and seers who use it based on the Unchanging Changer's will. In an interview he gave to *The Renewal Journal* before his death, Dr. White spoke against those who try to control and manipulate the Spirit's power and even called doing so witchcraft.

There has to be a balance somehow. A place where we acknowledge the Holy Spirit as God without trying to control His power ourselves. I wonder what would happen if we believed in the Holy Spirit, that He is God, that He is always with us, and that one of His jobs is to be our Helper as we live our life on earth? It's kind of scary if I'm honest. It makes life seem a little less my own, which is probably the point. But despite the fear and against the independence of my heart, I have to wonder, What if we are missing out on something amazing?

You might be thinking that it doesn't matter which member of the Trinity we pray to because the three persons are all the same God. And while I don't think it matters to God, I do think it matters to us. My life has been rocked by realizing that the Holy Spirit is with me. Praying to Him seemed almost wrong at first—which is silly because I say that I believe He is God, just like the Father and Jesus—but now I love it. It makes the literal part of my brain connect somehow with the spiritual part. Maybe it's because I know that God and Jesus aren't here on earth, even though I believe they can hear me. But the Holy Spirit, He is literally right here. And when I recognize that and talk to Him, it does something to my heart and my faith.

This is the space where we move past theology, beliefs, and even Scripture, although we don't let go of them. The place where we have to either choose to believe in a real God who is with us in a tangible, active way that literally changes our lives, or not. It's a scary leap past simple religion into a new reality. A reality where I am not the center of my own life and where the world doesn't revolve around me. But it's also a reality where seemingly anything is possible and where a Force much larger than myself whispers, guides, and leads if I will listen and let Him.

RECOGNIZING THE HOLY SPIRIT AS A REAL, POWERFUL, UNMANIPULABLE PART OF THE TRINITY COULD CHANGE YOUR LIFE.

15

WALKING THE AWKWARD MIDDLE WAY

When my friend Rachel invited me over to her family's fall
harvest party, I had no idea I'd be running into people from my
past. Or that there would be an awkward stare down over the
bonfire. Although Rachel and I had both grown up under the
influence of the same cultic organization, her family had always
been on the fringe and missed a lot of the craziness I experienced. Still, we had a bunch of mutual friends—something I
unfortunately forgot.

I hadn't seen these people in at least five years and let's just
say a lot had changed. For me, that is; they looked exactly the
same. It was kind of surreal. Maybe no one would recognize me.
Maybe they would think I was an unknown worldly soul in need
of conversion. Rachel couldn't let that happen.

I was warming myself by the bonfire when I realized that
I knew the woman directly across from me. She didn't notice
me until my dear friend loudly announced, "You remember
Christy Mills, don't you?" Then the woman's icy glare swept from
the tips of my jean-clad legs to the top of my short hair. I've

never felt so judged and condemned in my life, but I managed a sheepish smile.

"Hello, Mrs. So-and-so. How are you?"

Sometimes I still feel like I am getting glared at—only this time it's from two sides of the bonfire. I no longer fit in with traditional conservative Christians, but I also don't fit with more progressive types either. Maybe you can identify.

I initially heard the phrase *Via Media* from my good friend Alexis as we talked theology over bagels and coffee. *Via Media*, or the Middle Way, was first used religiously by Anglicans to refer to the Church of England as a middle way between the extremes of Roman Catholicism and Puritanism. I guess people have always been good at extremes.

I love the *Via Media* because it's where I seem to fit best these days. I'm muddling around somewhere between the extremes of the right and left—religiously, politically, socially. I refuse to compromise my historically orthodox view of the Bible and Christianity. But I also refuse to go along with the religious traditions of cultural evangelicalism. I want to passionately love the people God has created, and I want to hold to the actual truth of His Word at the same time. It's an awkward place, and kind of messy, and I definitely might get stuff wrong, but I'm okay with that. It's not that I'm compromising, I'm choosing to hold truths in tension. I've settled into the belief that tension theology is the place where truth lives.

Here is a story that might help you understand what I mean. A generous friend gave a pastor's family a slightly used trampoline, but it required set up. Hoping to make his children happy, the pastor began to assemble the trampoline. After putting the poles together to create the frame, he started connecting the springs to the side. As he made his way around the trampoline connecting sequential springs, the pastor suddenly realized that the mat was too small for the metal frame. Even though he tugged and pulled with all his might, he could not get the other side of the trampoline to connect. Feeling frustrated, the pastor removed all the springs to start over. As he took time to think, he decided to attach one spring on the first side before moving to the opposite side to attach a spring on that side. It worked.

When all of the springs were attached on one side, the pastor did not have enough force to connect the opposing side. However, with only one spring attached, it was possible to also attach the opposite side. In this way, he moved around the trampoline and was able to attach all of the springs with equal tension.

We can apply this story to theology and to our own ways of thinking. Many truths in the Bible require tension theology. Even though they don't always make logical sense, we must hold on to two opposing truths. The same is true in the way we think and the positions we take. Although popular in religious thinking, real life is rarely black and white. What if, instead of merely operating in *either/or*, we began to accept a *both/and* way of thinking?

Is God holy and just or loving and merciful? He's both. Predestination or free will? It's both. Is God three or one? He's both. See how this goes? It doesn't always make sense to our finite minds, but that's it. We are the creation, not the Creator. It's okay if we don't understand it all. In fact, if we can explain everything about God, then our god probably isn't the real One. There is much truth that needs to be held in tension.

What if actual truth can be found in the middle ground rather than in taking sides? What if this is the Narrow Way that Jesus not only talked about but personally walked? Is it possible to walk the Awkward Middle Way with Jesus? I think so.

I want to dialogue with people who are different from me. I want to learn from people I disagree with. I want to hold my perspective with an open hand. While at the same time continuing to believe in a very big, very real, incredibly amazing God who knows it all. Grace and truth—that is the goal in my pursuit of the Awkward Middle Way. I want to hold tightly to truth in one hand and grace in the other. I want to be like Jesus.

It's been amazing to find more middle-way muddlers lately. David Bennett, author of *A War of Loves: The Unexpected Story of a Gay Activist Discovering Jesus*, often shares that he feels this middle-way awkwardness. After David published his book, he received condemnation from both sides. Conservative Christians were upset because he calls himself a gay Christian and identifies as LGBTQ, and more progressive believers were upset because he affirms an orthodox Christian view of marriage and sexuality and is choosing to be celibate. He can't win. And yet, there are many people who have joined David in the Middle Way and are celebrating his journey with him.

Sometimes this journey can be lonely. But together we can be a tribe, a family. We might get glares from both sides of the bonfire, but that's okay because Jesus got a lot of glares too. We can figure this out together in humility, giving plenty of grace, and understanding that it's not really us-versus-them and rarely is anything actually black and white.

∎ | ∎ ∎ ∎ | ∎

Imagine we are taking a walk on a warm summer afternoon and we start to feel hungry. Across the street, we see an old-fashioned ice cream shop that advertises thirty-six flavors of homemade ice cream. Our mouths begin watering as we imagine fresh waffle cones. Scampering across the street, we open the door to the sweet tinkle of a bell. In all their homemade glory, thirty-six beautiful containers of ice cream are resting in a case behind a glass window.

The shop is quiet. We don't really notice the tables of silent people hunched over their bowls of ice cream because our eyes are focused on the menu. How in the world are we going to choose a flavor? Maybe they will let us have two different kinds.

We step toward the case and stare dreamily at the swirls of fudge, raspberry, and peanut butter. We comment on the thick fudge ribbon making its way through the creamy green of mint chip. Then we hear a voice.

"Would you like chocolate or vanilla?"

We look up from the ice cream case to see the employee staring at us. Puzzled, we wonder if we heard them right. "Excuse me?"

"Do you want chocolate or vanilla ice cream?" They ask again.

We are very confused. There are thirty-six different flavors of ice cream. Why do they want us to choose between chocolate and vanilla? We look at each other and shrug.

The attendant is still staring at us. "You should pick chocolate. We all eat chocolate ice cream here. Vanilla is for bad people."

Now we are really confused. "But I was hoping for mint chocolate chip," you stammer.

"Mint chip is basically vanilla. And you can't have vanilla. Only stupid people eat vanilla. How about chocolate?" Neither of us really likes chocolate ice cream, but we are starting to feel intimidated.

"Mackinac Island Fudge?" you ask slowly. "It's got chocolate in it."

"That's vanilla ice cream!" The attendant shouts. "Vanilla ice cream is wrong! Only terrible people eat vanilla ice cream. Don't you understand?"

"Butter pecan?" you whisper.

The attendant glares at you. In a cold voice, they slowly say, "If it's not chocolate, then it's vanilla. Vanilla is bad." Ice cream has lost its appeal and we decide to leave.

This crazy story is an extreme illustration of black-and-white thinking. When we believe that there are only two options and one of them is wrong, we are thinking in black and white. We see this way of thinking everywhere in our current culture. If you don't think exactly like me and my people, then you are wrong. There is no room for disagreement or discussion, no openness to hearing a perspective that is different, and no willingness to acknowledge that other people have reasons for their beliefs.

Growing up in my religious cult, I didn't know any different. This is how we thought. Obviously, we were right and the rest of the world was wrong. We had the hidden knowledge and secret wisdom. We understood the keys to success and blessings. Other people might mean well but they were deceived. Except that it was really the other way around and we were the deceived ones.

The black-and-white thinking that I see these days—especially from mainstream Christians—concerns me. It's on every side: conservative and liberal, progressive and fundamental. Everyone seems to think that there are only two options for everything. What people don't realize is that black-and-white thinking is dangerous. I know from personal experience.

Black-and-white thinking isolates us. We always think that our perspective is correct; it's our perspective, after all. But in reality, our perspective is warped because of our biases, experiences, personalities, and so on. When we exclusively surround ourselves with people who think like us, our biased perspectives are confirmed. We are right and everyone else is wrong.

Honestly, if we are going to have a more accurate understanding of life, we need to get to know and listen to people who are different from us. We need to hear the heart of who they are, the experiences they have had, and the reasons they think and feel the way they do. Reality is found within a combination of different perspectives.

When we only think in terms of black and white, we create enemies. If there are only two options, then life quickly becomes us-versus-them. Supposed truth and safety is found within the comfort of our tribe. Anyone who doesn't think like us is viewed with suspicion. We do not see the complexities of other people's humanity, and we ignore their stories and experiences. We are quick to bestow motives on them based on our own opinions and not their actual intentions. Most people have legitimate reasons for their perspectives, whether or not we agree with them.

Often, black-and-white thinking is based in fear. We are naturally afraid of things we do not understand. This fear can easily be exploited by people who want to control us. Most differences are not bad, they are just different. When we are consumed by black-and-white thinking, our fear keeps us from exploring or pursuing people who have differences. That fear traps us within our own narrow perspective. Fear is not from God. We need to evaluate our fears and discover if they are truly rational or not.

Finally, black-and-white thinking only benefits those in power. This is true in a religious setting, a political one, and anywhere in between. Those in power love to promote black-and-white thinking because people who think like this are easier to control. If we went back to the ice cream illustration I started with, who is benefiting in that scenario? The makers of chocolate ice cream. Who benefits in a religious system? The guy in charge of the church, cult, or organization. Who benefits in politics? The media and the people in political power. Black-and-white thinking is not helpful for the minions. We would be much better off connecting with all sorts of people with various backgrounds and beliefs. Our own opinions might be strengthened or changed as they are challenged, but we will be free to learn from one another in a healthy way. We will be free to love people like Jesus loves them.

It's easy to assume that our perspective is the correct one. But we are all flawed and broken. We each come with preconceived ideas and prejudices. If we are going to see accurately, we need each other. We need multiple perspectives from various angles. We need the Holy Spirit to illuminate the way. The early church was filled with people from different sides: Jews and Gentiles, men and women, slaves and masters. The apostle Paul reminded the new church in Ephesus that in Christ they were all one despite their differences. They were all saved by the same Jesus, all reconnected to the same Father, and all indwelled by the same Holy Spirit (Ephesians 2).

MAYBE TRUTH IS FOUND IN THE AWKWARD MIDDLE,
IN A BALANCE BETWEEN TWO EXTREMES, WITH A VARIETY OF PERSPECTIVES.

CONCLUSION

A few years ago, I got in a stupid online argument with a woman about my Instagram bio. We should never have been following each other in the first place, but we both signed up for this *following frenzy* so that we could have more followers and get noticed by a publisher or something like that. She was very conservative, reminiscent of people I knew back in the cult days, and she decided that it was her job to correct me and get me back on the path of righteousness. At that point my bio said, "lover of Jesus and hater of religion." She messaged me to let me know that hate was wrong and I shouldn't use that word. Um, thanks?

She continued to message me to correct me for various things I said over the next few weeks. I was a bit miffed because she clearly wasn't my intended audience, and after a few pointless debates we finally agreed to mute each other. I told her she could delete me but she wouldn't because it was "against the rules of the following frenzy."

Shortly after I titled this book *Religious Rebels,* I heard a chorus of fake people in my head—who sounded an awful lot like that woman—lecturing me about using the word *rebels*. "Rebellion is

as the sin of witchcraft," they said. I was getting judged by pretend
people and I hadn't even published my book yet.

Rebellion is kind of a triggering thing to me. Back in my cult
days, obedience to authority was the most valued thing. You could
tell how godly someone was by how obedient they were. The
worst thing you could be was a rebel. I classified the other young
people in my church into two categories: the godly ones and the
rebels. People who conformed and people who didn't. Rebellion
was utterly condemned. It was as bad as witchcraft—the Bible
even said so. And then, as you know, I became a rebel.

All of the noise in my head made me wonder, am I using the
wrong word in my title? So I looked it up. The phrase "rebellion is
as the sin of witchcraft" is the KJV translation of 1 Samuel 15:23.
The prophet Samuel had given King Saul a command from God
regarding the Amalekites. He was supposed to destroy everything, but instead Saul kept the good spoils of war and only destroyed what was worthless. When Samuel confronted him, Saul
made up an excuse that he'd kept the animals so that he could
make a sacrifice to the Lord. Samuel responds with this prophecy:
"Has the LORD as great delight in burnt offerings and sacrifices as
in obeying the voice of the LORD? Behold, to obey is better than
sacrifice, and to listen than the fat of rams. For rebellion is as the
sin of divination, and presumption is as iniquity and idolatry"
(1 Samuel 15:22–23).

I'm not rebelling or asking you to rebel against the Living God.
I'm pushing back against the extra, religious, man-made ideas
that have infiltrated Christianity. "Presumption is as iniquity and
idolatry," declared Samuel. There's an awful lot of presumption
going around these days. Both conservative and progressive thinkers presuming to know who God is and what He wants from us.
I'm rebelling against the ideas that we can decide who God is and
make up what we believe about him. I'm rejecting the false ideas
on both sides of the argument.

I'm pushing us to evaluate our beliefs and rethink our assumptions based on the fact that the real God exists whether we

want Him to or not. He is who He is and always has been, despite our opinions, feelings, or desires. We don't get to decide who God is, we get to discover Him.

Saul did his own thing and then tried to justify it by claiming he was making sacrifices to the Lord. But God, through Samuel, calls him out and gets down to the heart of the matter. God doesn't want our outward actions; He wants our hearts.

It has never been about perfection or standards or behaviors. It's always been about a God who longs to restore us to Himself. "Listen," Samuel says. And if we listen, we will hear the beginning of a story, where people were created to walk with God. We will hear the end of a story, where people once again dwell with God in the new heaven and new earth. And we will hear the middle of a story where God came and lived with us. Jesus showed us who God was, took the consequences of the world's sin onto Himself, and offers free forgiveness and life to all who will take it.

We don't have to be people who conform to the religious norms, customs, and traditions of our day. We can be rebels who seek to know God for ourselves and believe that He wants to be found. We can join hands in the Awkward Middle Way where together we hold the mystery of tension and paradox. Where we offer scandalous grace while looking for truth. And where we attempt to follow the One who called Himself the Way, the Truth, and the Life. Come with me, friends. Let's keep seeking the real Jesus.

Made in the USA
Monee, IL
03 August 2023

40404238R00085